Scattered All Over the Earth

Also by Yoko Tawada from Granta Books

The Last Children of Tokyo
Memoirs of a Polar Bear

Yoko Tawada

Scattered All Over the Earth

translated from the Japanese
by Margaret Mitsutani

GRANTA

Granta Publications, 12 Addison Avenue, London W11 4QR

First published in Great Britain by Granta Books in 2022

First published in the United States in 2022
by New Directions Books, New York

Originally published in Japanese as *Chikyuu ni chiribamerarete*
in 2018 by Kodansha Ltd., Tokyo.

Copyright © 2018 by Yoko Tawada
Translation copyright © 2022 by Margaret Mitsutani

A CIP catalogue record for this book
is available from the British Library.

1   3   5   7   9   10   8   6   4   2

ISBN 978 1 78378 903 0
eISBN 978 1 78378 912 2

Offset by Patty Rennie
Printed and bound by CPI Group (UK) Ltd, Croydon, CR0 4YY

www.granta.com

MIX
Paper from
responsible sources
FSC® C171272

Scattered All Over the Earth

I spent that afternoon lying on the sofa, hugging a cushion, watching TV with the volume turned down. Rain gives me a peaceful feeling. There's a stepping-stone path out front leading to a small park, and I never get tired of listening to the patter of rain falling on stone blending with that soft squishy sound of water seeping into the ground.

It wasn't the rain that kept me inside that day. I like strolling along by the canal, stopping for coffee or at a used record store on the way, or going down to the town square, working my way into the crowd around a hot dog stand to see if there's anyone I know waiting for one of those garish red sausages on a bun. But that day I just wanted to relax, and avoid doing anything much. As I turned my head so I could look out at the gloomy Copenhagen sky, I felt the silver light beyond the clouds start to glow inside me.

Doing nothing is harder than you'd think. Usually when I can't stand it anymore I escape to the internet, but that day just the thought of the blue screen put me off, the kind of light that drags everyone out onto a bright stage whether they want to be there or not. On that stage, blinded by spotlights, I'm a fake star. Ridiculous. Better to turn on the TV. I can lie on the sofa and watch the performers without feeling like they're watching me. I flipped through comedies that weren't the least bit funny, popular songs with an extremely limited vocabulary, ads plugging some kitchen utensil you'd use once or twice and then forget about. Then I came to one of those foodie shows, a tour of Danish restaurants.

Denmark is definitely the world's easiest country to live in, probably because we're not fussy about what we eat. You always find the Mafia and corrupt politicians in countries full of gourmets obsessed with food. We should admit that the reason we have clean politics and safe streets is that we don't care about taste or stuff like that and quit making silly gourmet TV shows, but for some reason on that day there was a boring show called "In Search of Denmark's Most Delicious Hot Dog." I must have dozed off watching it because I didn't even notice when the commercials were over and the next program started. When I opened my eyes I saw a panel of guests in the studio with a moderator who seemed very excited, going on and on. Gradually I realized that the panelists were all people whose countries no longer exist.

The first one, shown in close-up, was a German woman teaching political linguistics at the University of Copenhagen. The "German Democratic Republic," where she was born and raised, was now extinct. That's the country we used to call East Germany. Looking puzzled, the moderator asked her a question.

"The two countries were united, so you can't really say that either one disappeared, can you?"

"You don't understand. The country where I used to live is now gone."

"But can't you say that West Germany is also gone? Why does only East Germany no longer exist?"

Taking a deep breath, the woman started shouting into the microphone, so loud the sound was breaking up. Thank god I had the volume turned down low.

"After reunification, people's lives in the West went on as usual, while ours in the East changed radically. Textbooks, prices, TV programs, working conditions, even our holidays—

everything was adjusted to the West. We were suddenly like immigrants in our own country—where we'd been born and bred. Furthermore, historians in the East were told that the theories we had based our life's work on were worthless; we were driven from our posts."

This was much too heavy for relaxing to, but when I went to change the channel I couldn't find the remote. I'd taken it with me when I went to the bathroom a while before; maybe I'd left it by the sink. Since I was little I've had this habit of taking the remote with me when I go to the toilet, to make sure my parents didn't change the channel while I was away. Not so much because I wanted to see whatever was on as out of fear that my father would change the channel and my mother would get so mad at him she'd start smashing plates on the floor again. My mother wasn't fussy about what she watched, she just couldn't stand it when my father treated her as if she wasn't even there. My parents got divorced when I was fifteen, and I've been living alone for years now, and still I'm taking the remote to the bathroom … kind of depressing, really.

Getting up off the sofa to go get it seemed like a lot of trouble, yet I was really getting fed up with this program. While I was still wondering whether I should change the channel a man from the former Yugoslavia, a woman from the former Soviet Union, and a few others came on and said their bit for the cameras.

I listened to them, getting more and more irritated. They sounded almost proud of coming from countries that didn't exist anymore. As if that somehow made them special. We're not living in the Kingdom of Denmark anymore, so couldn't you say we've lost our country, too? Our ancestors had a sprawling kingdom that encompassed Greenland, but now we live in this one tiny country on the edge of Europe. That change didn't happen in my lifetime, but couldn't you say I'm the second generation of people who lost their country?

Actually, I'm sure our official loss of Greenland has something to do with my mother's strange affliction. Otherwise, she wouldn't always be going on about Eskimos as if they were her own children. Now she's paying tuition for a young Eskimo guy who's studying to be a doctor. I'm her own son, but when I want to go abroad and ask her for help with travel expenses she'll turn away and say something like, "Sorry—don't have any to spare right now."

I suddenly remembered I'd promised my mother I'd go over to her place for dinner that night. Going out in the rain was too much trouble. I decided to text her and say I'd caught a cold. If I phoned her she'd immediately know I was lying.

While these thoughts were running through my head a close-up of an entirely different sort of face appeared on the TV, and I slid off the sofa for a closer look. There used to be a popular anime called *The Cosmos Where Rain Never Falls* and she reminded me of the heroine. Apparently from an archipelago somewhere between China and Polynesia, she'd come as a foreign student, planning to stay for just a year but then a couple of months before she was supposed to go home, her country disappeared. She hadn't seen her family or friends since. Hearing that I swallowed hard, as if my mouth was full of lemon juice, but she just calmly went on talking. Her face was like the sky with the northern lights—bright yet dark. What really got to me, though, was the language she was speaking. I could understand it all right, but it wasn't Danish. It was much crisper, more staccato. For the first few seconds I thought it might be Norwegian, but no. It sounded closer to Swedish, but definitely wasn't that either. I was staring at the close-up of her mouth on the screen as if I wanted to kiss it, which was embarrassing, so I turned away for a minute, and when I looked back again I thought I saw a resemblance to that Icelandic singer Bjork when she was young. Could this woman be speaking some Icelandic language? She'd said she was from an island. Iceland is an island, too. But what about the geographical position? True, global warming is melting the arctic ice, making new oceanic currents, but you never hear anything about Iceland being swept all the way over toward China and Polynesia. So what language was she speaking anyway? The moderator must have been wondering the same thing. "Tell me," she asked, "what is this language you're speaking so fluently?"

For the first time, the woman smiled. "homemade language," she said. "no place to return. in gothenburg studied, but couldn't extend. so to trondheim went. one-year scholarship. spring, summer, autumn, winter quickly passed. what to do? trouble, but found job in odense. again moved. recent immigrants wander place to place. no country obliged to let them in has. not clear if they can stay. only three countries I experienced. no time to learn three different languages. might mix up. insufficient space in brain. so made new language. homemade language most scandinavian people understand."

"Wouldn't English work as well?"

"english speaking migrants sometimes by force to america sent. frightening. illness have, so in country with undeveloped healthcare system cannot live."

"Do you want to stay in Denmark permanently?"

"yes. hoping denmark afloat stays, not to bottom of sea sink."

I'd planned to do nothing this Sunday afternoon, but now my heart was pattering like a small drum. I felt a rush, like a street performer when a crowd starts to gather. The name *Hiruko, J.* flashed across the bottom of the screen.

What a strange combination of sounds. Three vowels ... Like Enrico in Italian, but that's a man's name, and wasn't there a similar Hungarian name? Eniko, a woman's name—maybe her country had historical connections to Hungary. Thoughts roamed the prairie of my mind like Huns on horseback.

"What kind of work are you doing in Odense?"

"storyteller at märchen center. stories from long ago to children tell."

"But you're very young. We'd expect someone much older to be telling folktales."

"everything from yesterday disappears, then yesterday into long ago transforms."

Breathing in several grammars, she was melding them together inside her body, and then exhaling them as sweet breath. Listening to those strange sentences, I stopped worrying about whether or not they were grammatically correct, and felt I was gliding through water. From now on, maybe solid grammar would be replaced by some new grammar, more liquid or air-like. I had to meet this woman. Not only meet her, but stay close to her if I could, and see where she went from here. I'd never felt this way before. Or called a TV station, either. I knew the station had a number you could call, but I'd never imagined using it myself.

"Hello, I'm a graduate student studying linguistics at Copenhagen University, and I was wondering if it would be possible to meet the woman called Hiruko who is appearing on your program now," I said. "I'm researching immigrant languages, and I'd very much like her cooperation. For a national research project."

The person on the other end didn't sound the least bit suspicious: "When the program is over, we'll ask her if she's willing to meet you. Please tell me your name and the official title of your department at the university. You'll have to wait until the program ends, so it will take a while, but we'll call you back."

I put down the receiver and went back to the TV to find that Part One with the panel of guests was over, and they were well into Part Two, with three specialists talking about vanished empires, the Romans, the Ottomans, the Yuan Dynasty. The first was a historian, the second a historical novelist, and the third a deep-sea archaeologist. I didn't even know such a profession existed, but apparently he dives under water to examine the re-mains of villages that were submerged when a dam was built, or Pacific islands that have sunk into the sea. He said that some-times when he's diving he'll hear a woman singing, or see a pale, headless corpse float up from the bottom.

"But you mustn't lose your cool, no matter what happens," he went on. "When you panic it messes up your breathing, so even if there's no problem with the oxygen tank, you can't breathe." The man had black hair, so shiny it looked wet, and red lips. Up-set, perhaps, that this handsome explorer was hogging all the at-tention, the historian cleared his throat and, like a ship's captain, took the helm and steered the conversation off in a completely different direction.

"Even when an empire sinks to the bottom of the sea," he said, "it doesn't disappear from history because it lives on in memory, from generation to generation, and then somebody decides they want to revive it. But isn't there something frightening about the idea of bringing an empire back to life? Of course it's fine to fix something that's broken, to restore it to its original condition. But doesn't the idea of *reviving* an empire bother you?"

The sort of "revival" he was talking about reeked of old-fash-ioned nationalism, which was certainly worth thinking about, but knowing I'd probably be meeting Hiruko soon, I went to the mirror and ran my fingers through my messy hair, trying to make myself look more presentable. Then I went to the dresser, picked out a clean shirt and fresh trousers, and had just finished brush-ing my teeth when I saw that the moderator was now seated fac-ing the camera, blinking with an "in conclusion" sort of look, which I thought must mean the end and then the music started up again as the camera panned aimlessly above the studio like a bird. The names of everyone who had appeared on the program fell like raindrops from the top of the TV screen to disappear, sucked in at the bottom.

I waited for about twenty minutes, wondering if my request had been pigeonholed, but one of the nice things about living in a small country is that you're rarely ignored. Another few minutes and the phone rang.

"Hello," said the voice on the other end, "this is the television station you were kind enough to call this afternoon. Ms. J says she'd like to meet you. If you'll come to the studio right away, she'll see you in the lobby." It was a different person this time, a man with a rather high voice, telling me just what I wanted to hear. I grabbed my raincoat with the advertising slogan ULTRA-LIGHT, WRINKLE-FREE, COMPLETELY WATERPROOF YET LETS YOUR SKIN BREATHE printed in big letters on the back in place of a logo, pulled on my waterproof cycling slacks, stuck my feet in my waterproof sneakers, and jumped on my bicycle.

I wasn't exactly lying when I said I was a graduate student in the linguistics department. For the past two years I've been involved in a three-year project to help young immigrants learn about Danish life through computer games, getting research funds and living expenses from the government. Though I don't think this sort of research is exactly meaningless, my conscience bothers me so much I sometimes get toothaches, or pains in my back. It would be okay if I was really into computer games, but, while secretly despising them, I made myself sound like a sympathetic spokesman for youth culture when I filled out the project's application forms. "Computer games" became my ticket to an easy, healthy lifestyle sponging off the government, knowing all the while how many young people get hooked on computer games and end up losing their jobs, getting fat on a diet of fast food, or start suffering from insomnia or diabetes. You can say you want a classless society, but once you've boarded a big, safe ship, it's hard to screw up the courage to switch to a dinghy. If things went on this way I'd get lazier and more depressed by the year, and maybe wind up sick like my mother. Before that happened, I wanted to take a year off and travel through Africa or India—some place with lots of languages to study. I didn't have much money saved up, but in most of the world the cost of living is so unbelievably low that with some careful planning I'd probably be able to manage a long trip. I might get by for six months or so just on my savings. And I was hoping to wheedle a little money out of my mother. But the moment I saw Hiruko's face, I lost all interest in that trip I'd been planning. The key to my puzzle was in this puzzling young woman. I'd never once called a TV station, or had the courage to set out to meet someone out of the blue. Suddenly I was so bold it seemed my whole personality had changed.

I passed through the security check at the broadcast studio entrance and gave my name to the receptionist in the lobby, who told me to wait in the visitor's corner. I was absentmindedly watching the stream of people go by when I saw a face I thought I recognized. That thin old man in the bow tie, smiling like someone who enjoys setting intellectual traps: that's Lars von Trier, I thought, but just at that moment a women I assumed was Hiruko was coming from the opposite direction. She had an odd way of sliding across the floor, not lifting her feet at all. When she looked up at me she stopped dead, as if her weight was centered in her belly.

"How do you do?" I said. "My name is Knut, and I'm studying linguistics."

"name feeling of intimacy gives."

"Actually it's an old man's name. My great-grandfather was apparently a wonderful person, so my mother just had to name me after him."

"great-grandfather also linguist?"

"No, he was a leftist Arctic explorer."

"among arctic explorers also leftists and rightists exist. linguist knud knudsen also your ancestor?"

"Unfortunately, no. I was really surprised when I saw you on TV today. That was a live broadcast, wasn't it?"

"yes. in your country live program without incident. your country fearless when guest suddenly sounds antidemocratic. your country with such incident naturally can deal."

Hiruko was sometimes hard to follow, but when I stopped to think, it seemed like maybe that was because I just wasn't very bright. Not that I think I'm particularly stupid, but after I smoke pot, I'll suddenly go all foggy in the head for days afterward. Like there's this idea right in front of me but my brain's too sluggish to grasp it—that sort of frustration. I couldn't tell whether the strangeness I felt listening to Hiruko was because of the dope or thanks to this entirely new kind of grammar she was using. But any sort of distance between us was purely due to language—on a personal level, I felt as if I'd known her since we were children.

"Are you living in Copenhagen?"

"no. in odense. but today single room reserved, so at wrist-watch looking unnecessary."

"Well then, can I take you to dinner? As a budding linguist, there are lots of things I want to talk to you about."

"to most people linguist not interesting job. to me linguist equals diamond." Hearing her say that made me so happy my heart did a back flip.

"What kind of food do you like?" I asked her. "How about Finnish home cooking—sushi, for instance."

"sushi not finnish."

"Are you sure? I always thought it was Finnish. There's a sign in the Helsinki Airport that says 'Welcome to the Country of the Three Wonderful S's.'"

"three s's?"

"Sauna, Sibelius, Sushi."

"not sushi, sisu. sushi entirely not finnish. i alone say, no one will believe."

"Well, I believe you," I assured her. "Shall we go? Do you have an umbrella?"

The rain had lifted, and the evening sun was tinting the clouds orange. For the Copenhagen sky, this was first-class service. I had promised to have dinner with someone else, I now remembered. Someone whose first name had dropped out of the picture, replaced by the privileged title Mother, the moniker under which she rules the inside of my head. As Hiruko and I walked along the canal, the evening sun glinted off the water like bits of gold dust.

"I can't get over your making up your own language. When you say made-up language, what I think of mostly are computer programming languages. Once I considered developing a theory for the language that's used in interactive computer games, but I gave it up because it's more a mathematical problem, basically different from what I think of as language. I studied Esperanto, too, but not for long. Just unlucky, I guess. There're lots of good Esperanto teachers, but the one I ended up with had terrible pronunciation. We used to talk about it behind his back. 'This must be the Paris dialect of Esperanto,' we'd say. It's an artificial language made so that people from all over the world can talk to each other, but with this teacher, the only ones who'd understand us were the people in our class. We would have been better off studying French. But you don't blame your troubles on anyone else, and all by yourself you've perfected a language you can use to communicate with people all over Scandinavia. That's really something."

"not perfect. my present situation equal to language itself. after one month less like norwegian, more like danish possible."

"If you stay in Denmark permanently, do you think your homemade language might turn completely into Danish?"

"unclear if immigrants in one place permanently can stay."

"I'd be really happy if you'd say Danish was more beautiful than any other Scandinavian language."

"pronunciation difficult because soft, mushy. now soft, mushy things eating while danish pronunciation practice."

"And all this time you haven't spoken your mother tongue at all?"

"mother tongue people not easy to meet. where all are i know not. little by little, planning to look for."

"How are you going to look for them?"

"after broadcast, many emails and phone calls came. so many places to look."

"Oh, so I wasn't the only one who called. I'm kind of disappointed to hear that."

"tomorrow in trier umami festival held. umami from my mother tongue originated. going there, some mother tongue person might meet."

"Can I go with you? I'm interested in languages from countries that have disappeared. Actually, this is a research topic I just thought of today, but it's starting to feel like something I've always wanted to study."

"trier good place for such research. center of holy roman empire, now extinct."

"The Holy Roman Empire isn't so interesting, now that all the native speakers of Latin have died out. You, on the other hand, are still young and full of life even though your country no longer exists." I thought I saw a shadow pass over Hiruko's face when I said "full of life," though I may have been imagining it.

Ever since we'd left the studio, we'd been talking as we walked down the street side by side. This is basically what she told me, although I may have gotten some of the details wrong.

Hiruko grew up in a high-tech village; they had electronic sensors buried under the roads that could detect snowfall, so hot water, apparently redirected from local hot springs, spurted out of tiny holes whenever it snowed. That kept the roads from ever getting blocked with snow. The roofs were heated, too, so snow melted as soon as it fell. Hiruko's grandmother said she needed to shovel snow or she'd get stiff all over, so even at age 100, she used to look for back alleys that weren't equipped with sensors so she could shovel the snow there. Her shovel would rise so lightly you'd have thought the cloud god was pulling it up from the sky by an invisible rope, then toss its load of snow exactly on the spot her grandmother was aiming for. All that snow, piled up in the same place, looked like a castle made of sugar. As a child, Hiruko never got tired of watching her grandmother shovel snow.

By the time Hiruko got that far in her story, my favorite sushi restaurant had come into view. When I saw the big sign out front with its picture of a Moomin, I knew I wasn't wrong after all.

"See—sushi is Finnish."

Hiruko shrugged her shoulders. "moomin to my country as exile came," she said, "finland between ussr and western europe in difficult balance was caught, great stress for Moomin loss of weight caused. to restore round body shape moomin exile became. as lover of snow, in my area lived."

"What's that area called?"

"hokuetsu. official prefecture name niigata. rule requiring use of prefecture name was made. that rule everyone broke. niigata no one said. hokuetsu everyone said. moomin everyone loved, because gentle, domestic, plump, almost hairless. very popular type of man, on TV every day appeared. but when cold war ended, moomin back to finland went."

"And why was that?"

"about old age worried. unlike finland, in my country pension not so much paid."

Inside the restaurant the air was hot and steamy; several people were already seated, having dinner. I pointed my chin toward an empty table by the window, and Hiruko nodded. The menu was new: it still had a list of different kinds of fish, but now each had from one to five stars beside it. I called a waiter over to ask him about it.

"What do these stars mean?"

"They indicate degrees of pain."

"Degrees of pain?"

"How much pain each species felt while it was dying after being caught. Fish caught in a big net die slowly, writhing and struggling. Those caught one at a time are immediately euthanized by more compassionate fishermen with a bang on the head. Our customers are free to choose."

I saw a hint of a smile on Hiruko's face.

"Now that human rights are totally protected," I said in defense of Denmark, "we're moving on to animal rights."

"all fishermen truth only tell? certain?"

"When the safety net covers everybody, no one has economic reasons to lie any longer, so people stop lying."

Salmon was by far the cheapest fish on the menu. There were rumors that too much growth hormone had been poured into the salmon farms in the Baltic Sea, causing such a population increase that the salmon had started eating each other. Since only the biggest and strongest survived, they kept getting bigger and bigger until you even heard about salmon the size of whales leaping out of the water. When people ate salmon raised on Baltic fish farms, their reproductive capacity was greatly stimulated as well; there were stories about couples coming home after eating sushi and heading straight for the bedroom to have sex. The women always had at least twins or triplets, but also quintuplets, and even way beyond that—you could find pictures on the internet of ten or twenty tiny fetuses in some woman's womb, all breathing through their gills. So I definitely didn't want to order salmon. Tuna's on the verge of extinction, and I'd been avoiding shellfish ever since that time I got food poisoning. I saw a fish called hamachi on the menu. A funny name that sounded sort of like "How much." I decided to forget about what they tasted like and order by name instead. A friend of mine, a literature major, once said you can see menus as a literary genre.

"There's a fish called 'Ça va.' Tako—that must be singular for tacos. Suzuki sounds cool, like the car."

"new model suzuki you saw?" Hiruko asked, surprised.

"No, not new. Though a friend of mine has a used Samurai, so old it's falling apart."

When we'd finished ordering, Hiruko told me more about her childhood. Bored with the snow-free roads, the kids always wanted to go deep into the mountains to play. But with the paths, trees, paddy fields, and everything else buried in snow, there were no landmarks. Worried about their kids getting lost, the parents had them wear kanjiki (snowshoes) outfitted with a computerized navigation system. Kanjiki were invented long, long ago, during "The Age of Writing with Rope"—that probably means before they had written language. Though we don't get enough snow in Denmark to need special footwear, I wore snowshoes once when I went deep into the Swiss mountains to research Rhaeto-Romance languages (minus the computerized navigation system, of course). The computer on Hiruko's snowshoes not only told kids which way to go or where deep crevices were hidden that they needed to avoid, but could also have simple conversations. Hiruko says that looking back, she now sees that that part of the program was utterly useless.

"Kanjiki-san," she'd ask, "where can I find a snowshoe rabbit?"

"I do not know," would be the answer. "May I help you with anything else?"

"Kanjiki-san, why does snow fall?"

"It takes too long to explain, so ask at home. Otherwise you will freeze to death."

Snow made a lot of trouble for the grown-ups, but to Hiruko winter was an exciting time, when her father got together with the neighbors and dug out a snow tunnel to school for her. There were lots of winter events, too. As drama was popular in that part of the country, they'd build a stage out of snow for Snow Troupe Musicals and Snow Kabuki performances. Though plays sometimes ran for over three hours, no one had any trouble remembering their lines. Hiruko had classmates who were discovered by casting agents and went on to careers as actors in the big city. And for some reason, almost everyone in Hiruko's country considered cities to be superior to rural areas, so even the words "the country" had negative connotations. This cultural climate led one man to devote his entire life to an outrageous plan to utterly transform the rural region where he lived, so that it wouldn't be "the country" anymore. He was undeniably dedicated and industrious. But too much dedication and industry can create terrible problems for the people around you. Because a mountain range was the only thing separating the northern district where Hiruko grew up from the big city, this man decided to remove that obstacle and connect rural to urban by scraping off all the mountaintops with a bulldozer. He believed that if he could level the mountains off in this way, the whole area would be swept by humid winter winds blowing in from the Communist Bloc, and snow would no longer fall. He bought a huge bulldozer with public funds and set to work, which was fine as far as it went, but leveling the mountains got to be so much fun he couldn't stop himself, and since the waters were rising due to global warming as the mountains got lower and lower, finally the whole island, completely flattened out, sank into the Pacific Ocean. Hiruko says it's possible that this is why her country vanished. When you hear someone talk about losing her country it sounds like a national tragedy, but what made Hiruko angry was the destruction of the mountains she'd loved. She couldn't care less about the nation. She just can't forgive the politicians who'd had no respect for the mountains.

While she was telling me this sad story, Hiruko's voice got so loud that people at other tables started giving us funny looks, so I picked up my cup of green tea as if I was making a toast and sang a little song to smooth things over. Hiruko's face softened as she put some wasabi into her soy sauce and stirred it around with her chopsticks.

Then I asked: "You are going to Trier tomorrow, aren't you? Is it really okay if I come along?"

Hiruko nodded, not the least bit wary. The smaller the country, the less time it takes to make friends.

"morning flight to luxembourg reservation i have. from luxembourg bus."

I called the waiter and had him make a reservation for me on the same flight. When I was an undergraduate I used to make reservations on my Smilephone, but a friend of mine, a year ahead of me in grad school, told me that a waiter will do anything you ask.

While we were eating matcha ice cream for desert, I said that matcha must come from Spanish, like macho, but Hiruko shook her head and said, "no. I alone say, so no one will anymore believe. but tomorrow one alone perhaps two will become." Her voice, though quiet, was full of hope.

CHAPTER 2   *Hiruko Speaks*

I got the phone call on a Tuesday, the first sunny day in a long time.

I was staring absentmindedly out the window, wondering why I'd come so early that morning. I couldn't see far because the building next door was in the way. The smooth wall usually looked gray, but that day it was much brighter, like milk with a pat of butter dissolving in it. A delicious color, with a flag's shadow dancing over it. The flag billowed, rose up, and started flapping, swimming in the breeze until it drooped down and played dead. Then it would wake up and start swimming again. That reminded me of something I'd seen long ago. What was it called? *Koi-nobori*? Didn't *koi* mean love?

I'd been working at the center for three weeks. The way the sunlight had been shifting little by little all that time had made the shadow appear just where it was on the wall, I thought, amazed by how the celestial bodies had pulled me into their silent workings.

But what was the flag doing there? I could only see its shadow, so I didn't know what it looked like. Perhaps it was some country's national flag. A few days before, on my way to buy a sandwich at a neighborhood shop, I'd seen a sign for an embassy. Of a country so tiny and unpretentious it made me happy to know it was still around. I couldn't remember its name, though. I leaned out the window and twisted around, trying to look behind me, up and over to the side, but I still couldn't see the flag. When a chilly breeze slipped under my collar and started down my back I quickly pulled my head in and shut the window.

On the table was the stack of drawings I'd worked so hard on the day before, for my *kamishibai* picture drama. The first one was supposed to be a crane in a paddy field with its leg caught in a trap, but the bird's head looked like a sprouting onion, and the body was shaped like the head of a golf club. I'd worked on it for hours and this was the best I could do. The first time I must have made the neck too short and fat, because when my friend Dorethe stopped by for a look on her way home she asked me if it was a duck.

"Oh, it's a swan," she said when I'd drawn it over with a longer, thinner neck. I quickly added two long legs, and her face lit up like a candle.

"I see," she cried, her voice rising, "A stork? Or a crane?" and without thinking I grabbed her hand and shook it. Dorethe is Danish, so the crane, who doesn't appear in any of Andersen's fairy tales, must have been hiding in a drawer at the back of her brain. And since this drawing managed to drag the word "crane" out of her, I guess it's one of my more successful efforts.

I felt a tap on my shoulder and turned around to see Dorethe standing there. Her lush blonde hair, not tied up in a "horse's tail" as usual, flowed down in waves over her shoulders. Her long wraparound skirt had a pattern of fish scales.

"similarity to little mermaid," I said.

"It's cosplay, to cheer the kids up."

" 'cosplay' from my mother tongue comes."

"Cosplay is English, isn't it?"

"different. english language people costume to cos shorten. english parts in non-english way put together."

Knowing all too well that when I start talking about language I get so excited I can't stop, Dorethe quickly changed the subject.

"You're so good at drawing I really envy you." She wasn't joking, or being sarcastic—she really meant it.

I was so embarrassed I wanted to disappear, but if I accepted her praise without saying anything she'd think I agreed with her, so with a heavy tongue, I said, "in elementary school days, everyone more skill had. fine calligraphy, beautiful pictures classmates made. in drawing i was eternal two-year-old."

Her eyes widening, Dorethe bobbed her head up and down.

I don't remember actually ever getting a good grade in arts-and-crafts class. There were kids in my class who without a single lesson could handle a brush so well you'd have thought they were reincarnations of Hokusai. Yet hardly any of them wanted to be artists when they grew up. They probably went to work for some company like their parents and left art for the weekends, satisfied to hang whatever they'd done—an oil or ink brush painting, a watercolor, or maybe a woodblock or copperplate print—on the wall at home.

Since coming to Europe, though, I've noticed that drawing isn't an everyday thing here the way writing is. People seem to think that paintbrushes are for a genius like Munch—ordinary people are embarrassed to even touch one. As they see no connection between art and skill, they think that no matter how good a person is at drawing, she shouldn't do it unless she feels destined to be an artist. There might be something to that. Still, I don't see any problem with knocking off posters for the kids or making a sketch when they ask me to. Yet Dorethe and the other teachers never offer to help with the drawings for my picture dramas. Most people's handwriting isn't fit for the eyes of a professional calligrapher, so what's wrong with drawing pictures a real artist would consider worthless? Europeans must think of handwriting and drawing as two completely separate things. If not, why are they so ashamed of a lousy picture when their terrible handwriting doesn't bother them at all?

I was the one who'd suggested doing picture dramas for the children, telling them a story as I flipped over the illustrations for each scene, but since there was no one to draw the pictures, I had to do it myself. That was hard for me, although I had fun making up stories to illustrate. The first one I wrote was a sort of modern fairytale called "Tamagotchi-gotchi." It was about a baby thunderbird trapped in his egg, unable to hatch. His mother had taken so many supplements to strengthen the shells of her eggs that his shell ended up way too hard. To make things worse, after laying her eggs the mother bird was hospitalized with "blue bird," a kind of depression that strikes breeding hens, causing them to suddenly collapse from the stress of being forced to produce so many eggs. So the chick "Tamagotchi-gotchi" can't break the shell of his egg and come out into the world. Feeling sorry for him, the crows and seagulls come and tap at the shell with their beaks, but it's as hard as brick and they can't break it. Sometimes words appear on the shell, forming sentences like "What is the weather like out there?" or "Cold today, isn't it?" The chick's thoughts appear on the shell, like on an electric billboard. As you can tell from its name, the thunderbird produces a small amount of electricity in its body, which it uses to communicate with the outside world.

The children listened to my story with their mouths hanging open. None of them laughed, or even smiled. I was getting worried, wondering if they were understanding the story when a boy raised his hand.

"Is 'Tamagotchi-gotchi' the name of the shell," he asked, "or the chick's name?"

The boy's eyes were as bright as the sun sparkling on a lake, his long, thick eyelashes casting a shadow of intelligence tinged with sadness on his brown cheeks. Judging from his size, I'd say he was about seven. Afghanistan, Syria, Iraq—the names of countries flashed through my brain like pictures from a magic lantern.

Where had this child come from? Perhaps there was a country called Math, and that's where he was from. In Math, the walls would be covered with intricate patterns, each line embodying a mathematical principle, so that the moment a newborn baby opened its eyes, the lines would be carving paths to theoretical reasoning inside its brain. No wonder the sloppy lines I'd drawn without even considering the possibility that the chick and its shell might be separate entities had left this child puzzled.

Perhaps starting with a modern fairytale had been too ambitious. I would try a folktale next. When I closed my eyes and tried to remember the stories I'd heard as a child, the first one that came to mind was called *"Bakékurabe."* The *kurabe* part meant a kind of contest, but how to translate *baké* into Panska? I hadn't come across a story like this in Europe, about animals that can change themselves into something else. There are lots of different characters in Moomin, but not because they've gone through some transformation—they're different from the start and stay that way. I thought and thought, and finally remembered Ovid's *Metamorphosis*, from ancient Roman literature. That was just what I needed—a whole collection of stories about transformations. Since the word "metamorphosis" is from Latin, it might be rather difficult for the kids, but once they learned it they could use it in all sorts of situations. Immigrants don't have enough time to learn lots of words that can only be used in one situation each. It's better for them to learn how to use basic but many-faceted words from the time they're children.

I showed them a sweater of mine that had shrunk when I sent it to the cleaners, and said, "metamorphosis," then acted out growing cold toward a lover by putting my hand over my heart, saying again, "metamorphosis." I told them about going back to a town where I had once lived and finding it completely changed and sighed "metamorphosis," and pointed out that when Dorethe put away her mermaid's costume and then appeared

dressed as a witch, this was also "metamorphosis. D........," a word that could be used in all sorts of situations. I decided to translate "*Bakékurabe*" as "The Metamorphosis Olympics." This is how the story starts: "fox, genius at metamorphosis, in certain village lived. in neighboring village tanuki, cousin of dog, lived. tanuki also genius at metamorphosis." As most of the kids probably wouldn't know what a tanuki was, I thought it would be simpler to make it a close relative of the dog.

In the story as I remembered it, the tanuki changes herself into a human bride, and is feeling quite pleased with herself until the fox appears, transformed into a delicious looking manju. When the tanuki grabs for the manju she reverts to type, her long tail sticking out from under her bridal gown, and is found out. Though I could be getting this all wrong, there's no one around to correct me so I'll just have to tell it this way, not knowing whether it's a genuine folktale or my own version.

I was having a hard time with "manju" until I finally hit on the idea of changing it to marzipan chocolate. Children who've just arrived in Denmark probably won't know what that is. In fact, tongues that speak Arabic or Turkish might be more accustomed to the taste of sweets like manju, a pastry filled with sweet bean paste. We immigrants may never be able to taste those sweets again, though, so I decided to stick with marzipan chocolate. Only one problem: would a dog's cousin be fooled by marzipan chocolate?

When I showed them the picture of the tanuki with her tail sticking out as she grabbed for the marzipan chocolate, the children laughed and cheered. This story went over so much better than "Tamagotchi-gotchi" that I decided to give up on modern fairy tales for the time being and make some more picture dramas based on folktales.

The purpose of this Märchen Center is to help immigrant children learn about Europe through fairy tales. At first Danes volunteered to read stories to the children, but they'd recently realized that hiring adults who are immigrants themselves works better, and that having lots of different nationalities all mixed up together is more effective than having immigrants teach only kids from their own country, which gave me an opening.

When I applied for a job here after seeing a help wanted ad in the *Nordic Weekly*, I was still living in Trondheim, Norway. I had just found out that I wouldn't be able to stay on at the university. What's more, the country I was supposed to return to had vanished, so I didn't know what to do, or where I'd live. While I was reading that help wanted ad, I got the idea of trying to teach my homemade language to immigrant children. It's an artificial language that can be understood throughout Scandinavia, which I privately call Panska. I stuck the "ska" of Scandinavia on the end of "pan," which means universal. There's a kind of ethnic folk dance in Sweden called the polska, which sounds like it should be from Poland though it's actually Scandinavian in origin. I'm hoping my name for this language I've invented has the same sort of strangeness.

Panska was not made in a laboratory, or by a computer; it's a language that just sort of came into being as I said things that people somehow understood. Comprehensibility is what's most important, so with that as my standard, I talked as much as I could every day. This was my great discovery—that the human brain has a language-creating function. You don't have to pick out one language to study and learn from textbooks; if you just listen carefully to the people around you, picking out sounds, repeating them, feeling the patterns of the language as a rhythm that reverberates through your body while you're speaking, eventually they'll turn into a new language.

A long time ago, most immigrants headed for one specific country and stayed there until they died, so they only had to learn the language spoken there. Now, when people are always on the move, our language becomes a mixture of all the scenes we've passed through on the way.

There are also languages called "pidgin," but as they're always connected to business, they don't really apply to me. I have nothing to sell. The only thing I deal in is language.

While I was thinking about how I could tell stories to children in Panska at the Märchen Center, I hit on the idea of showing them *kamishibai,* or picture dramas. Showing them a picture for each scene in the drama would be much better than just telling them a story in words. I wrote something to this effect in my note with the CV I sent to the Center, and immediately got a letter back telling me to come to Odense for an interview. Of course I spoke Panska, and it didn't take even five minutes for the words "You're hired" to start blinking on and off in the interviewers' eyes.

The trouble with me is that the only thing I'm really good at is coming up with suggestions. "Why don't we try this?" I'll say, giving shape to things that don't yet exist, and then coloring them in, convincing people that my idea is the future they've been waiting for. In the country where I was born, people didn't think much of this sort of talent. Someone who worked hard but rarely spoke was considered much more trustworthy. A man who'd slogged silently away at some project for decades, then one day mumbled something like, "You know, I sometimes think that *this* might be what I've been trying to do all these years," would be regarded with awe. A young person who was always going on about new things to try or improvements to make, telling her elders how much better things would be if they'd leave everything up to her, on the other hand, would get hit over the head with a hammer of words. There was an old saying, "The nail that sticks up gets hammered down," and a game besides, called "Whack-a-Mole," invented just to give people practice at hammering down those pesky nails.

In Europe, nobody played Whack-a-Mole on my head when I started talking; instead, they listened, their eyes bright, telling me they wanted to hear more. At the interview, I spoke eloquently about what an excellent genre *kamishibai* was, and of the great benefit it would bring to Denmark. I could tell by the interviewers' shining faces that they were warming to me. Not one asked, "Have you ever made your own picture dramas?" When not only had I never made one, I'd never even seen one. I had only a dim memory of a storyteller I once saw in an old movie, selling candy to the kids crowded around him, then showing them pictures of scenes from "The Peach Boy" as he told them the story. I didn't want to lie, though, so I said, "my dream for *kamishibai* as big as elephant. my experience with *kamishibai* as small as mouse."

"That's all right," one of the interviewers replied. "You can learn through experience. It's the idea that counts. We'd really like you to show your picture dramas to the children at our center." Surrounded by smiling faces, I read the contract and signed it right there.

By the standards of my home country, my drawings were lousy and the stories I made up were far-fetched. Even so, I was sure that the children looking up at me now, their eyes sparkling like sunlight on water, were absorbing some global culture. There were plenty of people in my country capable of making *kamishibai* of much better quality, but they weren't here, or perhaps anywhere else either, so I had to do it myself, and I'd throw out my guilty feelings along with the marzipan-chocolate wrappers.

Having found myself a job, I was able to get a visa and settle down in Denmark, for the time being anyway. I remember hearing about "illegal aliens" on TV as a child, thinking they must be bad people from some faraway country, and yet now, if my luck gave out, I myself would soon be illegal. When you think about it, since we're all earthlings, no one can be an illegal resident of earth. So why are there more and more illegal aliens every year? If things keep on this way, someday the whole human race will be illegal.

That day the kids started arriving early. Half an hour before *kamishibai* time, that clever-looking boy who'd asked whether "Tamagotchi-gotchi" was the chick or the shell marched in and headed straight for the bookshelf, where he took out a picture book and started reading, standing up. A round-faced boy missing his front teeth who'd looked confused last time walked straight in today and plunked himself down in the front row, then gestured to other kids as they came in, suggesting places for them to sit. A little girl with a scarf over her head sat down next to him. More boys and girls seemed to be sitting together today. Lots of kids were wearing the same clothes they'd had on last time. And there were some newcomers. A boy hanging on his father's arm. A girl shyly looking down as a social worker brought her in by the hand.

A boy in the front row over to the left was watching a video on his Smilephone. Many people assume that all refugees are poor, but some of these children are from families escaping war and persecution, not poverty. It's true that many of them left their homes and everything they owned behind, but some managed to bring a little money and a few possessions with them, or have funds sent from their home countries. The boy with the Smilephone, who didn't look old enough to start school, was all dressed up in a smart jacket with a silk necktie.

Today I planned to tell them the story "The Crane Returns a Debt of Gratitude" but even if I managed to translate "a debt of gratitude," I doubted the kids would understand it, so I decided to call it "The Crane's Thank You" instead. A loom's much harder to draw than a crane. I wasn't sure I'd be able to explain how cloth is woven, and besides, would it even be possible to make crane feathers into thread? I finally gave up on the loom altogether and had the crane wife secretly pull out her feathers to make a down jacket. That was much simpler than having her weave them on a loom.

In my story, a man who marries a woman without knowing she's really a crane takes the expensive down jacket she makes for him into town, where he sells it for more money than he's ever seen. Just when I was telling the kids how happy the man was to be rich for the first time in his life, Dorethe came rushing in still dressed like a mermaid to tell me I had an urgent phone call. I said "sorry, back soon" to the kids, ran to the office, and picked up the phone to find that a television station wanted me to appear on a "serious" program the following week. I asked for details, and was told that a group of people whose countries no longer exist would be telling their stories. They had heard about me from a reporter at a local newspaper and I remembered that just the week before someone had come to interview us about what we were doing at the Märchen Center.

I refused as politely as I could. If people saw me on TV, someone might recognize me when they saw me later, walking around town and use that as an excuse to talk to me even though they had nothing to say. That would be an awful nuisance. Satisfied that I'd declined the offer, I was about to hang up but the woman from the TV station kept talking, gently yet very persistently. I would get a lot of money for appearing on the show, and the station would pay for my transportation and hotel as well. Besides, someone from my home country might be watching and contact me, she said, and that's when I started to waver.

"but next day to trier must go. preparations many. busy," I protested, but the woman assured me that the station would not only pay my way to Copenhagen, but also buy me a plane ticket from Copenhagen to Trier the following day.

By the time I said, "no airport in trier. to luxembourg fly," I was already leaning more than halfway toward appearing on the program. The woman didn't miss the change in my tone.

"Then it's decided, right?" she said, and hung up the phone.

Thrilled to hear I was going to be on TV, Dorethe wanted to know all about it, but all I could tell her was that the program would be live, and that I'd be going to a TV studio in Copenhagen next Tuesday—I had no idea how long the show would be or who would be appearing with me.

I went back to the room where the children were waiting, told them the rest of "The Crane's Thank You," sent them home, and then started getting ready for the following day. Though I'd chosen "Kaguya Hime" for my next picture drama, I didn't know what "Kaguya" meant and had no dictionary to look it up in. I would just have to translate it as "The Moon Maiden," but while I was drawing the first picture it seemed like "The Bamboo Maiden" might be a better title. The stalk of bamboo where the old couple find the shining girl should be her home, so why is she always talking about "going home to the moon"? Maybe Kaguya Hime was the child of immigrants. She was born in a bamboo tree on earth while her parents were living here, but unable to feel at home in her earthly environment, she's always dreaming about "returning" to the moon, where her parents are from. I thought of drawing a sequel, about Kaguya Hime when she is back on the moon. Because she knows only life on earth, the moon seems dull and barren, with no grass, flowers, trees, swallows, or cats. She remembers the flowers with all their colors, the songs of birds, and mammals—their smells, their warmth, their quarrels, the fun they have playing—and feels so homesick that she decides to go back to earth. I planned to draw the sequel when I returned from Trier. At the time, I thought I would be coming back to Odense right away. But although "Odense" has four letters in common with "Odyssey," I never suspected that this would be the beginning of the story of a long, long journey, in which I would play the central character.

Outside the Märchen Center there was a small stone court-yard with a statue of a little girl in the middle, also made of stone. She was standing perfectly still, looking as if someone had cast a spell on her just as she was about to strike a match, freezing her in place. Every time I saw her I was afraid she might start moving one day, and I would turn to stone.

I was glad I'd appeared on that TV program. Afterwards several people called in to say they had met someone who spoke my mother tongue. They all had deep, raspy voices, though, and when I asked how old they were they said they were in their nineties, and that the meetings they'd spoken of had happened long, long ago.

Another caller had harsh words for me. What sense is there in looking for someone who speaks your mother tongue, this person wanted to know. Why couldn't I be satisfied with the language I was speaking now, and concentrate on getting along with the people around me, helping them so they'd help me? That sounded reasonable enough.

But the next call was kind of creepy: "You should have a child right away to keep the genes of your tribe from dying out."

"Only right-wingers see the disappearance of their father-land as a crisis," another caller said. He had a point; it was the ultraconservatives, the exclusionists who were always moaning that if things went on this way the fatherland would go to ruin. I'd better be careful, I thought to myself. I hadn't meant to say my fatherland had gone to ruin. "Fatherland" and "go to ruin" weren't even in my vocabulary.

Some woman said we didn't need language anymore now that we have emoji, which seemed to me to be missing the point. If her son broke her favorite vase what would she do—draw an angry-face emoji for him?

"The smaller languages will eventually go extinct. Lifting children out of poverty is much more important," said another caller. Listening to all these people made me so tired the light telephone receiver in my hand started to feel made of lead. I finally stopped taking the calls myself, and asked someone at the station to answer the phone instead. They switched on the speaker phone so that I could hear the voices of an old couple say they felt so sorry for me they wanted to adopt me; then an enthusiastic stamp collector wanting to know if I had any rare stamps from a vanished country; and also a young boy eagerly asked if I had ever met a ninja.

I was about to go to the hotel for a rest when I was told that a linguistics student had called. Unlike the others, he wasn't interested in my vanishing mother tongue, but in the homemade language I was now speaking, so I asked them to have him come to the station.

When he finally arrived, I took an instant liking to this young man named Knut. I could sense his libido gushing out not toward me, but in the direction of language. In Europe, an unusual type. Most people here are still very interested in sex, either in the opposite or their own, so when they meet someone for the first time they inevitably ask themselves if this new person could be their partner, or if they're currently with someone, if he or she could take that partner's place. This seems to be purely theoretical—it's not as if they're seriously considering dating the person they've just met, but imply that these questions are always at the back of their mind.

In the country where I was born, though, sexual hormones have long been practically extinct. Men weren't expected to have hairy chests and arms, or to need to sleep with some woman at regular intervals, and women didn't have to have breasts like balloons, and always be wanting to have children.

That was the main reason why hardly anyone wanted to study abroad by the time I started to university. "You'll have an awful time in a place like that," my friends all said when I told them I was going to study in Sweden. And sure enough, on my first day at Gothenburg University, a boy from my seminar invited me over to his place. He gazed longingly into my face, his long eyelashes making him look like a movie star, and when he put his hand gently over mine I realized with a start that this must be what people call romantic love. When I quickly explained that in my culture sexual hormones had died out he stared at me as if I were a woman from the moon.

"Will your parents object?" he asked after some thought. He had probably seen some documentary about societies where parents choose their children's marriage partners, or forbid them to marry foreigners or heretics, and assumed I must be from somewhere like that.

"not parent problem," I said, "in my culture, no sexual hormones."

"That's terrible," he said, sounding genuinely worried. "What sort of disease is that? If you don't want to talk about it now I'll totally understand, but I've got a friend who's a doctor, so I'll call him tomorrow."

While Knut didn't seem entirely oblivious to sex, he didn't want to bother with anything too complicated or troublesome, was disgusted with his clinging, overprotective mother, and had a natural tendency to find eroticism in language. Just the sort of person I wanted as a traveling companion. When I met him, I had no idea how fundamentally our travels would change both of us.

We agreed to meet at Copenhagen Airport the next morning, and checked in together. Shaken by strong winds, the propeller craft trembled, moving up, down, and sideways as it climbed the stairway of clouds. Moving his fingers so fast I could hardly see them, Knut was sending a text message.

"cloud mode strict rule," I said to him.

"I have it on flight mode," he said. "I'll write my message now and send it later."

"who?"

"To the person I was supposed to have dinner with last night. I stood her up without contacting her."

"lover?"

"Sort of. Actually, she used to be my father's lover. She married my father, and then had me."

"one who in every language by word starting with m is called. mama, mother, mutter, mutti, maty, maman."

"Does it start with m in your language, too?"

"mama-haha we have. special kind of mama."

"My mother is also a special kind of mama. An Eski-mama."

"eski-mama?"

"That's right. My mother believes that she's the mother of all Eskimo children. Nobody says 'Eskimo' anymore because it's supposed to be racist, but in this case Inuit doesn't fit. The kids on my mother's mind are definitely Eskimos. A while back she showed me a photo album with portraits of one hundred people now living in Denmark, so naturally there were all types, including people with one Eskimo parent, say, or an Eskimo grandmother. The first face was very fair, with blond hair and blue eyes, but as you turned the pages the hair and skin got closer to the color of wheat and the eyes got darker until you came to thoroughly Eskimo faces. She'd intentionally arranged the pictures that way, so you couldn't tell where the boundary was. But I think it shows how unnaturally obsessed she is with race."

"album what purpose?"

"To show that we're all kinfolk. She probably wants to say that the Danish people can't be totally cut off from the Eskimos."

"denial of independence?"

"People like my mother acknowledge Greenland's independence, but are against cutting off aid. Like parents who can't stop meddling in their son's life even after he grows up. They want to recognize him as an independent person, but they can't just stand by and watch him screw up his life with drugs. What my mother calls 'responsibility' I call 'meddling.'"

I took another good look at Knut's face. His skin was so fair that any reddish patch stood out like a wound. Was I just imagining it, or did he look like he might be doing drugs? If it was only marijuana I didn't need to worry, because this flight wasn't headed for Singapore. I felt a little ridiculous, quickly making these judgments in my head. Pressing my forehead against the glass window, I saw castle walls surrounded by deep green on the ground below.

He suddenly entered my line of vision at the Luxembourg Airport's bus terminal where I was waiting for the bus to Trier. Round cheeks, hinting at the nicely shaped bones beneath—a truly delicious young man. The woman with him looked exotic, a type one rarely sees these days. Too short to be a Han woman, yet her skin seemed untouched by the sun, so not a native of the Mekong Delta either. Her straight black hair brushed her shoulders; seen at an angle from behind, the line from cheek to chin resembled that of an anime character, cute yet slightly creepy. She walked without lifting her feet, gliding along sideways as if she had no weight at all. The strangest thing was that I could almost see pictographs in her eyes, blinking on and off.

I remember learning about people of this type in a class on historical geography; how long ago, when our country India was called South Asia, they lived in a place that was also called Asia, but specifically Far East Asia. These Far Eastern people apparently shared a number of bizarre characteristics. One was an inability to distinguish between the virtual and real world: stories were told of people who, when severely beaten by an internet gang, would die of their wounds, and of youngsters in love with online stars diving into their computer screens, never to be seen again. There were even tales of laborers who worked eighty-hour shifts without sleeping, which would astound even our most ascetic yogis.

Taking another look at the woman, I saw a gentleness in her

face that did not match these outlandish stories of Far East Asia, but this may have been due to her being with the young man, who would surely melt the heart of anyone he stood beside. The language they were speaking sounded Scandinavian. They jabbed and caressed one another with words, one telling a joke that angered the other, then laughing together, exchanging little slaps on the arm, but never kissing or staring longingly into each other's eyes.

That day I'd come to meet ten students from India, gathering from various parts of Germany, to escort them by bus from the Luxembourg Airport to a hotel in Trier. If not for my tour guide duties, I would have been able to speak to that lovely young Scandinavian and ask him to tea. He did not look to me like a businessman. I thought he might be a budding scholar, studying ancient Greek literature, perhaps, or baroque music. And yet in his intelligent face, I thought I detected a trace of emptiness, which worried me. The emptiness appeared like mist, then vanished. But my long, deep relationship with a friend who'd surrendered his personality to hashish may have made me overly sensitive to such impressions.

Looking this way and that, apparently trying to find some point of interest in this dull bus terminal, the young Scandinavian finally discovered our group. Seven of the students I was to take to Trier were women, and three were men. While the men wore jeans with plain white shirts and yellow or black leather jackets over them, the women were in bright Punjabi dress with scarves around their necks, each of a different hue. Among the Europeans, whose clothing grows dark and drab as summer ends, we looked dangerously gorgeous.

Ever since I decided to live as a woman I've been wearing saris of varying shades of red when I go out. Not that I'm intentionally dressing *Indian*, but as German women of my generation hardly ever wear skirts I didn't want to wear one myself. And if I wore trousers as they do, I'd simply look like a man. Furthermore, I have always felt somehow that my heart must be made of red silk embroidered in gold. If I could only read the story woven in that golden embroidery, I'd surely know my destiny. I'll never read it, of course, but just gazing at the sheen of red silk is enough to satisfy me.

Though anyone can tell at a glance that I am moving to another sex, at the university no one ever mentions it. The same is true at parties. What they all want to know about instead is my sari. How do I wrap it around me, does it ever slip down, is it made of silk, am I wearing underclothing, aren't there more suitable shoes for a sari than my sneakers, so many questions, and I have such fun answering them because I do love to talk.

But the Scandinavian youth didn't seem interested in my sari or my sex—I overheard him say "Marathi." He must have seen the astonishment that undoubtedly showed in my face. Feeling an explanation was called for, I said to him in German, "You knew that we were speaking Marathi, didn't you? I am truly amazed. Many people here in Germany don't know that such a language exists. And even those who do assume it is a small language. Whereas in fact as many people speak Marathi as speak German."

"About a hundred million people speak German as their first language," the young man said in English with a friendly smile. "There are probably around three quarters as many Marathi speakers." I was searching for a reply when he stuck out his hand and said in English, "My name is Knut. What city are you from? Pune?"

"That's right," I said, taking his hand. Following his lead, I also spoke in English, "How'd you guess? You must know India well." Wanting to say more, I went on to tell him things he hadn't asked about. "Actually, once a year there's a gathering of Indian students studying in Germany, mainly for, you know, companionship and tourism, and because I live in Trier, this year I'm the host. How well I'll fulfill this role remains to be seen." Knut appeared to understand German although he didn't speak it well, which is probably why he switched to English. The woman, who had been looking back and forth between Knut and myself, asked in a quiet voice, "What is your name?"

"Akash. And what is yours?"

"Hiruko."

"Have you come for sightseeing?"

"We're going to Trier for the Umami Festival. There will be a dashi workshop at the house where Karl Marx was born. The cook lecturing there is called Tenzo, and judging from his name, he might be from my country."

Looking nervously around, she was speaking English in a voice I could hardly hear.

"Tenzo? A name I am hearing for the first time. And though I know nothing of the Umami Festival, I do know the house where Karl Marx lived. It's near the Porta Nigra."

When she heard that, the tension in Hiruko's cheeks relaxed. I suddenly remembered a beautiful Indian girl I once knew, named Dash.

"But what, may I ask, is dash?"

"Dashi? It's what makes the food you cook taste good. It comes from dried fish, or seaweed, or mushrooms."

"Is it the same as umami?"

"No, not the same. Umami's the flavor, but dashi's the substance. I think that's the difference, though I'm not exactly sure."

"So dashi is the total sound coming from an orchestra, while umami is the music."

The bus to Porta Nigra arrived, putting an end to our conversation. I had been hoping to find out more about their relationship, but the conversation had veered off on this tangent and I had wasted valuable time. Though Knut and Hiruko boarded the same bus as our group, they chose seats far away from ours.

While the bus was moving, I twisted my body around from

time to time to observe them, sitting in the back. Each time I move my hips, I feel my inner woman. Hiruko has the sweetness of apple blossoms, but none of the deep eroticism of marigolds. Knut's such a charming young man I want to embrace him. Watching them sit shoulder to shoulder, chatting away like old friends, I found it hard to sit still.

People from my country love to talk. Even when meeting someone for the first time they immediately start exchanging information about the university, their families, life in Germany, and as their enthusiasm grows, so does the volume of words. The bus was already buzzing like a beehive poked with a stick. Fortunately, the only other passengers were an elderly couple who were telling the students in the seat in front of them about a trip they took to India together when they were young. Though no one pays me any mind when I board a bus alone, a group of Indians riding together always results in a certain tension in the air. That's why guiding a group of my fellow Indians around Germany makes me nervous.

No matter how many times I see the Porta Nigra, I am overwhelmed. The hardness of stone, its heaviness, silences me. No nails or cement were used to hold the stones together; each one, heavy as a tombstone, has been kept in position for hundreds of years by the sheer force of its weight. Just thinking how long this has been a special place—ever since it was chosen as the location for the city's north gate in the second century—makes me dizzy. No matter how digital the world becomes, this heaviness exists only here, and no computer screen can hold it.

Looking up at the gate that loomed over them like a charred mountain, the students gasped in surprise and delight, posing in front of it, taking each other's pictures. Knut and Hiruko, apparently also seeing the Porta Nigra for the first time, smiled and stared. I sidled up to Knut.

"You know, there's a building in my country with a very similar atmosphere," I told him. "It's called Shaniwar Wada. That may be why I always feel comfortable at the Porta Nigra, as if I've come home."

His eyes half-closed, Knut repeated the words "Shaniwar Wada" as if tasting them, rolling them around on his tongue.

"Are the two buildings really so much alike?" he asked, his eyes bright with curiosity. "Is there some historical reason for the similarity?"

"I really don't know. Looking objectively at their shapes, perhaps they're not really the same, but when you get close, the stones give you the same sort of feeling. Stones you can depend on, that are worthy of respect, stones that make you feel secure."

Hiruko, who had been listening to us, spoke in a quavering voice, as if she were about to cry: "There were no big stone gates in the country where I was born. Houses were made of wood and paper, and they all burned down. Now everything's gone. Even if India and the Roman Empire are connected, I am all alone."

This lament of hers was so strange and seemed so out of place that I didn't know what to say. Perhaps her country itself had vanished. The thought of hearing any more was so frightening that I changed the subject.

"Why does your voice drop to a whisper when you speak English?" I asked. Though her voice was clear and carried well when she and Knut were speaking that Scandinavian language, in English it wasn't much louder than the sound of breathing. That had been bothering me for some time.

"I'm frightened," she said. "Twice at Scandinavian immigration offices they said I should move to America because I can speak English. I clearly wrote 'cannot speak English' on all the forms I filled out, so I couldn't figure out how those officials knew. Ever since, I wonder if there are spies nearby no matter where I am."

She looked so terrified I thought I should say something to cheer her up.

"I hear the policy of sending people to America has ended," I said in as bright a tone as I could manage. "Of course, non-English speakers have an advantage over English speakers. For staying here, that is."

"I do not plan to live in Germany," she answered, still sounding gloomy.

"Are you returning to your home country, then?"

"What is it that you call 'home country'?"

Just then, a group of policemen in dark green uniforms and black leather jackets walked past the Porta Nigra. Hiruko swallowed the words she was about to say and bit her lower lip. She seemed genuinely afraid they would hear her speaking English. This reminded me of something I had overheard while waiting in line at the student cafeteria. With Mexico's economy booming, Spanish speakers are now flooding in from California, greatly decreasing the West Coast's work force. And since China has stopped exporting goods, America must produce all its daily necessities domestically, but no one there knows how to sew anymore. This being the case, they're desperately trying to recruit immigrants who can speak English and are good with their hands. Europe, on the other hand, has developed a comprehensive welfare system that covers everyone, including immigrants, but with national budgets running low, they would rather have all the foreigners who can speak English move to America.

Fortunately, India has now reached the peak of its economic growth. While many Indians come to Europe to study or for sightseeing, no one wants to stay here and spend a life suffering from cold and a lack of spices. I myself am planning to return to Pune after I finish my studies.

If this strange woman called Hiruko really has no place to go, perhaps she is trying to entice Knut into marrying her so that she can get a Danish passport. Then she would be spared the fate of spending the rest of her days bent over a sewing machine in America, and could instead live surrounded by Scandinavian furniture, with no need to worry if she loses her job. Knut must be terribly naive—he doesn't seem to suspect her at all.

"When you said 'everything's gone' it sounded so awfully sad," Knut said to her. "Why not think of this as a new start? Maybe I'm not qualified to say that, though. But anyway, first you'll meet this guy Tenzo, and together you can remember all the words of your common language. Then you can make a dictionary." He was doing his best to encourage her, and in English, too, so he must have wanted me to hear and understand. What a lovely fellow. Lightly placing my hand on his back I turned him toward me and, pointing to Simeonstrasse, the street in front of the Porta Nigra, explained, "Right down this street is the house where Marx lived from the time he was a year old until he was about sixteen. I'll take you there myself. Please wait here for five minutes while I tell the students how to get to their hotel. It's easy to find—I'm sure they can manage without me."

Knut nodded, while Hiruko stared blankly into space—I couldn't tell if she was even listening. I went back to the students.

"Go straight until you come to a bridge," I told them. "When you've crossed the bridge turn right and you'll see the hotel. I'm off now, so let's meet at the university tomorrow at the appointed time." I then hurried back to Knut and Hiruko. The way young Indians walk, it would probably take them at least fifteen minutes to reach their destination. I knew perfectly well that telling Indians to walk that far is rude in the extreme. Some of the girls would expect to take a rickshaw any place farther than a three-minute walk away. But if they take as many taxis in Germany as they took rickshaws in India they'll quickly use all their scholarship money, and besides, to survive in Germany, they will have to walk. My German friends all love to go for a walk and often ask me to come along. Not just for fifteen or twenty minutes, either. They'll keep going for an hour at least, and in good weather as long as two without a rest. What's more, about forty minutes into our walk a friend will finally open his heart to me and confess, "I broke up with my girlfriend": without strong legs, you can't even make friends in this country.

After I had sent the students on their way the three of us started down the left side of the broad avenue in front of the Porta Nigra. Though I was supposed to be guiding them, for some reason Hiruko took the lead with Knut and myself following behind, so that we formed a triangle. With me in my sari, and Knut walking by my side, perhaps from a distance we looked like a heterosexual couple.

I am now actually changing into a woman, not only in dress. But as I don't want an operation or the hormones Western doctors love to prescribe, I am making the transition gradually, through many different methods—diet, meditation, exercise, breathing techniques, and chanting or copying the sutras.

Thrilled to be with Knut, I was walking on air, and sailed right past the building I'd been heading for, so we had to retrace our steps.

"Look," I said, "do you see that sign?"

Below the white wooden window frame on a pastel pink wall was an engraved granite plaque: "Karl Marx lived in this house from 1819 to 1835. Born in Trier, 5 May 1818." This was the first time I had noticed that though he was born in 1818, Marx only started living here a year later. How to fill in that blank year after his birth?

On the ground floor was a shop selling cheap toys, paper plates, notebooks, and candles.

One Euro Shop, the sign said. Hiruko read it aloud, and Knut burst out laughing.

"You know, a world where everything costs one euro doesn't

sound bad at all," he said, suddenly turning serious. "One euro for a car, one euro for ice cream—everything nice and equal."

"Is that what Marxism was?" Hiruko asked, her voice echoing loudly off the stone-paved entrance, causing all the passersby to stop and stare at us. One had a particularly piercing gaze. A policeman in plainclothes, perhaps. A sturdy fellow, but wearing such a big, loose jacket I couldn't tell whether hidden underneath was a muscular physique or just a fat belly. We instinctively turned to the stuffed hippopotami on display in front of the shop, feigning great interest in them. We figured they'd think that no one with a child, or maybe a niece, to buy a stuffed animal for could possibly be a terrorist. And apparently we were right, because the passersby now started moving again all at once, as if someone had pressed the play button on a video. He of the piercing gaze disappeared into the crowd. Hiruko, still nervous, whispered something to Knut, who turned to me and asked in English, "Are we back to the days when just saying the name Marx was enough to make you seem like a suspicious character?" I couldn't tell whether he was translating what Hiruko had said, or if this was his own question. Though his voice was intentionally loud, this time nobody stopped.

"Marx is a common name in this part of Germany," I replied, "so no one thinks anything when they hear it. There's a Marx haberdashery, and a Marx book store. Everyone knows that the Marx clan has been living in Trier for a long time."

"So does the Marx family also run this One Euro Shop?"

"Probably not, because it's a national chain."

"But is this really where the Umami Festival is going to be held?"

"I'll ask inside," I said, happy to be of assistance to Knut, and went into the shop alone. The narrow corridor was full of customers, but fortunately, there was no one at the checkout counter. The woman working there gawked at me, dumbfounded.

"Excuse me," I said politely, "but I hear an Umami Festival is to be held here today."

"Umami?" she asked with a frown. "What's that, some Indian god? We don't carry them here."

I knew from experience that women of this type, with false eyelashes, bright red lipstick, surgically enhanced breasts, and spike heels, tend not to view people like me, who are moving from one sex to another, very favorably. Still, since her attitude was neither condescending nor hurtful, I thought she might be on the liberal side. And what's more, she even surmised that umami might be the name of an Indian god, which shows a certain openness to foreign culture.

"So you have Indian gods other than Umami?" I asked, teasing her a bit.

"Of course we do," she answered. "They're very popular, you know. See those Buddha and Ganesh figurines over there? All just one euro." Ganeshes, painted blue, and golden Buddhas sat calmly on a shelf, holding their own among rows of Statues of Liberty and soccer stars, all about ten centimeters tall.

A bespectacled woman, a reader by the looks of her, then emerged from the back of the shop. I quickly decided she might be worth a try.

"Excuse me," I said, "but I hear that an Umami Festival is scheduled to take place here today."

"I told you," snapped the woman at the cash register, glowering at me, "that there's no such festival."

"Wait," said the woman in glasses, putting up a hand to quiet her colleague. "I heard about something like that, and I think it was today, but at the Karl Marx House Museum. A famous chef from some faraway country reveals the secrets of dashi, passed down since the middle ages—is that what you're talking about?"

So the event wasn't here after all, but at the museum. When I'd thanked the woman in glasses I returned to my companions and found them in the midst of a heated discussion, speaking that Scandinavian language. Wondering if it was a lover's quarrel, I was filled with hope for a moment until Knut turned to me and said in English, "Although Trier is in the Moselle Franconian group, the dialect people speak here is different from other villages in the region. That's because early in the nineteenth century Trier was taken over by Prussia, and the Prussian officials who came flooding in influenced the language—you can see that, can't you?" He was so excited his spittle was flying, but I was greatly relieved. He clearly had no interest whatsoever in Hiruko as a woman. And in exactly the same way, she tried to win me over to her side. "But don't you think the whole concept of dialect is out of date?" she asked, sounding just as overwrought as Knut. "When experts decide whether what people speak is independent language or just dialect there's almost always a political agenda behind it—you see that, don't you?"

"I am sorry," I apologized, trying to keep from laughing. "Linguistics is not my specialty, I do have a friend who's studying dialects, though, so I'll call him later. He has his own doubts about the concept—he even wrote a paper about it. 'You can't say it out loud,' I remember him shouting one time, 'but Luxembourgish is nothing more than a German dialect. Just because the vocabulary's different doesn't mean it's a whole different language.' He ended up roaring drunk that night. That really surprised me, for why should a man who calmly accepted his girlfriend's leaving him take to the bottle just because he lost an argument about dialects? But anyway, getting back to the Umami Festival, it seems it's not being held here, but at the Karl Marx House Museum. That's on Brückenstrasse, so let's go."

Perhaps Knut and Hiruko were still excited after their debate about dialects, for their faces were flushed and their shoulders heaved as they marched along behind me. The beating of their hearts must have set boilers burning red hot inside them, because when I looked off to the side for a moment they passed right by me, chugging along like two steam engines, striding on ahead. Perfectly in step. Considering how much taller Knut is, this was truly amazing. My legs kept getting caught up in the silk of my sari, making it hard to keep up.

The main street leading out from the Porta Nigra is always crowded, no matter what day it is. From shop windows, mannequins dressed in the latest fashions slyly watched the passersby. From time to time, I smelled the sinister odor of sausages grilling. Suddenly, Knut stopped.

"Are you hungry?" he asked me. I don't know why he asked me rather than Hiruko, but it made me feel as warm inside as if he'd hugged me.

"Yes, I am," I answered. "Let's have something to eat. I am a vegetarian—do you mind vegetarian food? These days, almost all German restaurants serve vegetable dishes."

"So Europe is turning into India."

"I don't know about that. Germans have many different ways of interpreting what counts as vegetarian. For instance, some places insist that beef stock soup is vegetarian as long as there's no meat in it. And there are even restaurants that serve chicken salad as a vegetarian dish on the grounds that chicken isn't really meat."

For the first time, Hiruko smiled at me. "I'd like to make you some delicious soup with kombu seaweed dashi." While I didn't want to put a damper on our budding friendship; I had to tell her the truth.

"There are various types of vegetarians," I said, "but in my family, we don't eat seaweed."

"I see," she said, her smile taking on a hint of sarcasm, "seaweed is always with fish deep in the sea, playing with them, caressing them, so I guess you can't really say it's vegetable."

"Let's go to an Indian restaurant," said Knut, putting a hand on each of our shoulders. He towered over us. Perhaps this was normal for Scandinavians, but he must have been about six and a half feet tall.

I took a deep breath, inhaling my joy at Knut's having suggested Indian food along with the air. "I know a place called Osho," I said. "It's a little out of our way, but their Satori Lunch is always good."

"Osho?" asked Hiruko, raising her eyebrows.

"That's right."

"Osho?"

"Yes ... is there something wrong?"

"The word *osho* comes from my country. It's what we call a Buddhist priest."

"No, Osho is the name of a famous Indian." Now I was getting irritated.

"No, osho is common noun."

"Osho is a proper noun, someone's name."

Standing between us, Knut tried to settle the matter. "Wait, let's consider this from a phonological perspective. First, just to make sure," he said, turning to me, "you're saying that Osho is a Marathi name, am I right?" This got me all flustered.

"No, it's probably not Marathi. This man was from a village somewhere in northern India. When he was born, he was given a different name. I can't remember what it was, though. Then when he achieved satori, his name changed, but to what, again I couldn't say. At the end of his life he was definitely called Osho, though. I heard that from my father. Pune, our hometown, was the center of his religious activities."

"Then it's possible he took a foreign word, a common noun, to use as a sort of stage name," Knut observed and, forced to admit he might right, I duly nodded.

As we got nearer to the restaurant Osho, I started worrying, but not about the name. I had not been there in several months.

Recently, restaurants I've frequented will go out of business, and before I know it they're replaced by coffee shops. So I was relieved when I saw the sign for Osho. The interior, done in mustard yellow, had no needless decorations, but the warmth and drama of the fabrics used for tablecloths and wall coverings kept the place from feeling sterile like the modern coffee shops that are popular now. What's more, the tables were arranged in such a way that when seated, one immediately felt safe, protected by the surrounding space.

Knut, too, seemed pleased. "This place has a really nice atmosphere," he said. "I've loved Indian food ever since I was a kid." Hiruko, on the other hand, was squinting suspiciously at a couple near the back. They were eating what looked like pizza. Though being nearsighted I wasn't able to see clearly, I nevertheless felt uneasy. I wanted to believe they were having chapatis with curry spread over them, but I'd never seen anyone eating chapatis that way.

A waiter dressed in white cotton brought our menus. On the first page were "Recommendations for Lunch," which consisted of three choices: "Satori Pizza," "Lotus Dream Pizza," and "Meditation Pizza."

"This menu is entirely different from the last time I was here," I protested, looking up at the waiter.

"Is that right?" he said coolly. "Then the last time you were here must have been quite a while ago."

"This is an Indian restaurant, is it not?"

"Of course."

"Is pizza Indian food?"

"All the dishes we serve here are popular at the Osho International Meditation Resort in Pune."

I was shocked. Knut, who could understand German, was listening with a broad grin on his face. Fortunately, he seemed more amused than angry. Hiruko poked him in the ribs, urging him to translate for her. I wiped the sweat off my forehead with the back of my hand and waved the waiter away.

Shouldn't the place where Osho gave sermons and everyone gathered to meditate be called an ashram? Resort sounded frivolous, infuriatingly so. And people were eating pizza there? Hiruko, having now heard the contents of my conversation with the waiter from Knut, was laughing.

"Pizza from a meditation resort?" she said. "Meditation pizza? That's really funny. Let's try it." Realizing how much all of this was troubling me, Knut reached over and placed his hand on my shoulder.

"It's all right," he said, comfortingly. "Italian or Indian—it doesn't really matter. After all, don't they say Marco Polo brought the idea for pasta back to Europe from Asia? That makes Italian pasta a kind of Asian food."

"But why should I have to eat the same pizza as the guests at a meditation tourist resort in Pune? And in Germany! It's so depressing."

"So now do you understand how I feel, just a little?" asked Hiruko. Startled, I looked over at her. Whatever resistance I'd been feeling toward her until that moment melted away.

The pizza, when it came, was ordinary, the sort you could order on the internet. On careful examination, the arrangement of the toppings bore some resemblance to a mandala, however slight. Knut took a bite.

"You can't express deliciousness using the first person singular with a transitive verb," he said, sounding perfectly serious. "That's always bothered me."

"Isn't it enough being able to say 'This is delicious to me,' in something like the dative case?" Hiruko replied, not sounding terribly interested, concentrating more on the back and forth motion of her knife as she sawed away at a slice of pizza. Still upset at being forced to regard pizza as Indian food, I didn't bother with such utensils, tearing off a slice with my hands instead and stuffing it into my mouth. It had absolutely no flavor. In the throes of violent emotion, one loses all sense of taste.

"First you become aware of the flavor, then you compare it with all your previous experiences, and finally, you connect it to the word 'delicious.'" said Knut. "Since all that takes place in the brain, shouldn't there be a linguistic form that matches the process? Doesn't the fact that you can only say 'This pizza tastes good, or terrible' show how impoverished our culture is?" He looked at Hiruko, whose eyes were fixed on the wall in front of her. She was staring at a poster for the Umami Festival at the Karl Marx House with today's date and the time, 7:00 p.m. What appeared to be two pictographs were written beside the time and date.

"So Tenzo is tenzo," she murmured. Knut burst out laughing.

"You're seeing two languages in your head right now." he said. "But when they come out of your mouth, they sound exactly the same to us. You'd laugh too if somebody said, 'So panda is panda,' wouldn't you?"

"Without seeing the two pictographs on that poster over there, I never would have remembered the word tenzo. It's a very special kind of word."

"You mean it's not the name of a five-star chef?"

"Maybe he's using it as stage name. But it's actually a common noun."

Remembering that embarrassing argument about whether osho was a proper or common noun, I looked down while Knut continued his conversation with Hiruko in English.

"So what does this common noun tenzo mean?"

"Tenzo is the person who prepares food in a Zen temple."

"I thought Buddhist priests traveled from place to place, begging for their food."

"In small Buddhism that may be true, but in great Buddhism, it's different. All Zen temples have a kitchen."

"What do you mean by small Buddhism?"

"There are two kinds of vehicles, small and great. In this case, great doesn't necessarily mean better."

"So it's like a truck versus a tricycle. I wonder which would be the great vehicle in Christianity, Protestant or Catholic."

Little by little I was starting to like Hiruko, which surprised me. "And are you a Buddhist?" I asked her.

"No, I'm not a Buddhist. I'm a linguist."

"Is that a religion?"

"Not really, but languages can make people happy, and show them what's beyond death." At this, Knut gently brushed Hiruko's cheek with the back of his hand. Though it lasted just a moment, there was a sweetness in the air, as if they were lovers.

"The festival isn't until 7:00," I said, looking down at my lady's wristwatch. "We have a lot of spare time until then."

"I want to see the Roman Empire," said Knut, beaming with excitement.

"Since you're an extreme vegetarian, who doesn't even eat seaweed," Hiruko said, a bit sarcastically, looking down at my watch, "I thought you must be vegan, but I see your watch strap is made of cow's leather." This I simply had to protest.

"You're wrong," I said indignantly. "This is synthetic leather. I even have a certificate showing it's not cow's leather. Would you like to see it?" This wasn't a lie. While I was still in India, I wore a watch with a cow's leather strap that my uncle had brought me as a present from Europe. But when I came to Germany I sold that watch, and bought one with a synthetic leather strap instead. People were always asking me why an Indian would have a leather watch strap, and explaining why got to be too much trouble. Which reminds me that my mother once told me that Gandhi ate meat while he was growing up in India, but switched to a completely vegetarian diet after he went to study in England. I wonder if that's really true. I have been a vegetarian since I was a child, but it seems my parents often ate fish when they were young.

"You know," Knut said, "I've wanted to come to Trier since I was a kid, to see the Roman ruins. But I'm awful lazy, and I hate traveling more than anything, so I just had never gotten around to it."

"You hate to travel?" asked Hiruko, as if she couldn't believe what she was hearing.

"That's right. Unlike you."

"I've never even thought about whether or not I like traveling. I'm like a leaf floating down a stream."

"That makes me a bug that can't get off the leaf," said Knut. "Thanks to you I've come all the way to the Roman Empire." He lifted his glass of mineral water as if it were wine.

"Prost!" I said, lifting my glass also. "Welcome to the Roman Empire. May we never be slaves who are fed to the lions." I slapped Knut on the shoulder and smiled to show him he could leave everything up to me.

"There's one more favor I'd like to ask of you, Akash."

"What's that?"

"Could you reserve a hotel for us? We've got no place to stay tonight."

"What sort of hotel would you like?"

"We can't afford anywhere that's too expensive. And we don't want to go too far away, either. A hotel in this area would be nice."

"There are several hotels on the way to the Karl Marx House Museum, so let's stop in and ask." Knowing I'd find out whether they were going to take separate rooms or sleep in the same bed when they made the reservation, my heart beat a little bit faster.

Knut had finished his pizza and was now leaning back in his

chair, bringing his right hand up to his lips as if smoking a ciga-rette. Hiruko was still eating, very slowly.

"How is the taste?" I asked her.

"In the country where I was born," she said, looking very sad, "it was very important for food to be delicious. And there was an old saying, 'It's the sick who really know what tastes good.'"

"The Dutch and the Scandinavians don't bother much about how food tastes, and look how tall they get," laughed Knut. "Maybe worrying too much about flavor stunts your growth." He then turned to me. "What are you studying at university, Akash?"

"Comparative culture. Comparative literature has long been popular, but what I want to compare is films. I'm afraid I am still hesitating at the entrance to this discipline, however."

"The movies … Language is much more interesting without the pictures," he joked, winking at me. But then again perhaps he wasn't joking after all. We were all in good spirits, laughing and poking each other like children as we left the restaurant.

Whenever I see the Kaiserthermen (Imperial Baths), they look to me like a group of elephants with their trunks together, having a good gossip. The part above ground is beautiful, the way the stones change color as the sun moves across them, but what I really wanted to show Knut and Hiruko was under-ground. Tunnellike passages run all through the baths like a maze. Standing in silence, surrounded by the dampness of an-cient stone with the light pouring in like milk, you hear footsteps and voices of people who are not there. They're the citizens of ancient Rome—you see them wrapped in white cloth, talking while they sweat in the sauna, scrubbing their bodies, and their voices echo off the stone in a blur of sound.

"Had I been born in ancient Rome," I said, "I wonder whether I would have been a slave drawing water or a merchant talking shop in the great bath and then stopping in a bar for a drink on the way home."

"Caste," whispered Hiruko.

"No, not caste. According to Roman law, a slave with enough money could buy his freedom, but you could never change your caste."

"So you can change your sex, but not your caste," Knut said, suddenly bringing up a topic he hadn't even touched on until now.

"That's right," I said, a little flustered. "Our bodies are always changing, from moment to moment. In these baths the ancient Romans surely felt that. They'd have unwanted body hair plucked away, get their hair and nails cut, enjoy a massage to loosen their muscles. The body changes when we sweat in the sauna or drink water. And that's not all. Even our brains change sex every second—depending on the book we're reading, we become men or women. There was a library here in the great bath, and a room where you could hear lectures as if you were at the university."

"Bath University? Sounds good," Hiruko said. We continued walking through the tunnel. There was apparently an exit up ahead, for we could see light at the end. And walking toward us, with the light at her back, we also saw a human figure. Although we couldn't see her face, she was obviously tall and well built, and the sun shining behind her made her blonde hair look like flames. This is like watching a performance of *The Ring of the Nibelung*, I thought to myself.

CHAPTER 4   *Nora Speaks*

I was putting up a sign by the front entrance that said "Umami Festival / Dashi Workshop Canceled" when I noticed a man I didn't know, standing to my right.

"Canceled, eh? That's too bad. I was looking forward to it."

His gray hair neatly combed, his flannel collar turned up a little, he stood there with his hands in his jacket pockets looking very casual, as if he were just passing by on an afternoon stroll, but on closer inspection I saw his shoes, as shiny as two black beetles, and the perfectly straight creases in his freshly pressed trousers. He looked as if he wanted everyone to know how healthy he was. He was so sunburned he might have just returned from a week's vacation in Majorca, although the new layer of red rested uneasily on the surface like an inflammation, with the skin underneath still resisting it. His hands being darker than his forehead, I took particular notice of the white circle around his third finger. He must have been wearing a ring while he was on vacation. The absence of one now suggested that a divorce had been discussed on the plane on the way home. But the myriad details of this stranger's appearance, all begging me to read them, were getting tiresome, so I turned away and checked my sign to make sure it was straight.

"The lecturer who was supposed to lead the workshop can't come," I replied in a slightly shrill yet official tone. "All international flights have been canceled due to political turmoil in the country where he is now," I added, angrily pressing down with my index finger on the stubborn air bubbles left in the cellophane tape.

Peering into my face, he repeated, "Political turmoil?" pronouncing each syllable slowly and clearly in the condescending manner of a high school teacher trying not to act like an authoritarian. *"Political turmoil" isn't quite the expression you want*, he seemed to be saying, *but rather than correcting you I'll let you try again.* Perhaps this man was a retired Gymnasium teacher. If so, his monthly pension was undoubtedly much higher than my salary. No matter how comfortable his life was he must still miss making students listen to him, and now, after trying to educate his wife, and working so hard at it that she got fed up and left him, he spent his days wandering the streets, looking for fresh victims. Putting an end to my theatrical daydreams, I stepped back to take another look at my sign. Remembering that I'd used a water-based marker, afraid it might rain, I looked up at the sky to see a crow fly overhead, slowly flapping its wings.

"And from what country was this lecturer supposed to be coming?" His voice was now as soft as a pussy willow, so I couldn't very well ignore him.

"From Norway, where he's staying now. All international flights have been canceled, so he isn't able to come."

"I don't believe Norway is a country with much political turmoil. There was nothing about it in the newspaper."

With time and energy to spare, perhaps this pensioner reads the newspaper cover to cover; maybe he even cuts international news articles out and files them according to country. My anger at being treated like one of his students made me more talkative.

"Surely any country has young people who turn to terrorism to get attention from the media."

"But such a terrorist attack surely would have been in the news."

He definitely had a point—the uncertainty I had been suppressing came bubbling up to the surface again. That morning, when I'd picked up the phone and heard Tenzo gasp out a snowstorm of words, "No international flights...I can't come," it hadn't occurred to me to doubt him, my head was too full of the urgent necessity to let everyone know that the event had been canceled: people tired after a long day's work, but still thirsty for something new; some may have turned down an invitation just so they could come to this workshop. I could imagine how downhearted they'd be on arriving here, full of anticipation, only to find the word Canceled across the closed doors, which was beyond their power to change. Fortunately the head of the museum was away on vacation, but having begged him about hosting a festival until he'd finally agreed, now I didn't know what I'd say to him.

"Anyway, it's a shame it's been canceled. As I said before, I was looking forward to it. Just think—an Umami Festival, and at the Karl Marx House. Actually, there's been very little research on the relationship between gustation and poverty or social class. There is, however, a method of measuring poverty by calculating the percentage of food expenditure in total household expenses. Do you know what it's called?"

There he was, at it again. I suppose after years of teaching you never lose the habit of regarding everyone as a student.

"You can't understand the new poverty using Engel's coefficient," I answered coldly. "The percentage a poor family spends on food today is quite small. They can buy cheap processed foods; for instance, with the catchphrase *Geiz ist geil* (stinginess is cool) ringing in your ears, you can buy meals to heat up in the microwave for only one euro.

"They'll definitely make you sick if you eat them every day, but they don't let that bother them. That's what it means to be poor now."

"So you're hoping to develop the palate to the point where

people realize how awful that sort of food tastes, and in turn, what a truly miserable situation they are trapped in, am I right? People used to look down on the gourmet life; it's so terribly bourgeois. But the gourmet life is not your goal; when you planned this event you were aiming for a new proletarian art revolution, one that starts with people probing the depths of flavor in their own lives, a revolution that begins on the tongue. A splendid idea. You and I may well be thinking along the same lines. Won't you have a cup of coffee with me sometime? Allow me to introduce myself. My name is Reichmann. Reinhart Reichmann. Please call me Reinhart."

I wasn't listening anymore. The words "I don't believe Norway is a country with much political turmoil" were clanging around my empty head like a temple bell. Could my chef instructor have been lying about all international flights being canceled because he didn't want to come back to Trier? Even to myself I was now using the term "chef instructor" because calling him "my lover" would have been too painful. I wanted to go to him right away, to talk to him directly. He'd said he was going to some sushi restaurant in Oslo. I'd written it down and put the paper in my pocket, but now it wasn't there. Perhaps it had all been a dream. Just as I lifted my right foot to take a step I stumbled as if I'd been standing on a stool with a loose leg, making the whole thing sway from side to side. The man suddenly stretched out his arms to catch me, asking, "Are you all right? Do you feel ill?" His voice was much deeper than before. He'd lowered his body as well, to catch me, which I didn't mind except that his elbows were pressing down on my breasts, which reminded me that the phrase "to catch someone in one's arms" also means "to deceive."

It all started about a month ago. I was strolling through the Kaiserthermen as usual, wearing loneliness like a cardigan with a jacket over it. I'd stopped dropping in at bars on my way home, perching on a stool at the counter like a yellow parakeet drinking Campari and soda, red as a sunset, while I waited for some man to start a conversation; deftly refusing my colleagues' invitations to parties, not even bothering to check what movies were on, I'd head straight for the Roman Empire as soon as I got off work. There are ruins wherever you go in Trier: the Roman Amphitheater, the Constantine Basilica, the remains of the Imperial and Barbara baths, the Roman Bridge over the Mosel River, and the Porta Nigra. Among the many baths, only the Kaiserthermen—grand enough for an emperor—had the power to expand my shrunken imagination, small enough to fit into a coffee cup, and pull my miserable everyday life back up into the great, blue sky.

I once read about a garden somewhere on the other side of the globe where flowing water is expressed entirely in stone, without a drop of moisture. Just once, I'd love to see an ocean or a waterfall made of stone. Now that the Kaiserthermen is a ruin, hot water no longer flows through it, but staring at the stone walls I sometimes think I hear splashing from the distant past, which for some reason sounds like *japon, japon*. Then the tension in my body melts away, and I relax. Not that my work is particularly strenuous. Nevertheless, to any employee, work is to some degree a place where strangers pull at you from right, left, above and below, pinching, rubbing, and generally making a mess of you from morning to night.

When I reached the Kaiserthermen that day a month ago, a tiny crack opened in the dark, heavy, rain clouds, sending a ray of light down to shine on the ruins. The light looked strange, and very pale. The ruins are stone walls and underground passages, with no roof. Although there used to be an entrance fee, since the most recent renovations, now anyone can get in free. With young people losing interest in history, this is city policy, to give them easy access to the ruins. Yet the young seem to prefer clubs and concrete parking lots to the Roman Empire, for they never come here to meet their friends. Most visitors to the ruins are tourists, many from faraway countries. On sunny days I sometimes hear the rhythms of a foreign tongue behind me, and while I'm still trying to figure out whether it's a Slavic language, or Chinese, or one of the Romance languages, it fades away into the distance again. On that day, though, the ominous, stormy skies must have frightened even the tourists away, because I didn't see anyone.

From below I heard sad but piercing cries. For a moment I thought it was a coyote, but that was probably because I'd been watching a film at home the night before with scenes of a Canadian forest. There are no coyotes in Germany. As I listened, straining my ears, a strange language emerged from those cries, like a song. I couldn't understand what it meant. Melancholy vowels dyed the air blue. I walked down the crumbling stone steps into an underground passage, following the voice farther and farther into the interior. As if escaping, the voice grew fainter and fainter until it finally disappeared, but when I stopped moving a different sound tightened the air around me. *Japon*, the sound of a large drop of water falling into a puddle, and another *japon* about three seconds later. As if drawn into the tunnel I started walking again, and when I turned the corner, several yards ahead I saw a young man lying on the ground, his body curled up like a shrimp. "Hello," I called but there was no answer. Between us the stone floor was black and shiny. If it was wet I might slip, so bending my knees and lowering my hips, I crept slowly towards him. I could see his backbone through his white T-shirt; his sneakers were old and worn. His face was hidden by his long hair. I reached out once but pulled back in hesitation, then screwed up my courage and touched his warm shoulder.

"What's wrong?" I asked, raising my voice. "Are you sick?" His rounded back straightened up into a sitting position, and his long, black hair slipped down over his shoulders, revealing the face of a young man in his midtwenties.

"Shall I call a doctor?"

For a moment the silence seemed to bind us together.

"No, I don't need a doctor. I was just resting a while because I sprained my ankle."

Though his face looked exotic, he answered in fluent German. The words came out naturally, even after a bad fall, so he was obviously used to speaking our language. It would be rude to ask someone that fluent where he was from, but he seemed so very foreign, not only in appearance, but in general atmosphere as well. He seemed relaxed, yet not reckless. Graceful yet solid, ready for anything. Hoping for a hint to his past, I asked his name, and the answer he gave me was "Tenzo." A name I had never heard before. The order of "e" "n" and "o" was the same as in "Fernando." Perhaps he was from a country that had long ago been ruled by Spain. The Philippines? South America? But I detected a hint of Siberia in his face. A strength that can take cold into the body as nourishment.

I don't want to even think about a person's country of origin if I can possibly avoid it. It seems to me that people who have to know where everyone is from have no confidence in themselves. But the harder I try not to think about it, the more I find myself wondering who comes from which country. There are so many pasts: one that starts out, "I come from X." Or in the country where a person went to elementary school. Or in a colony. There must be something wrong with me, asking for a name to learn about the past, when it should be the beginning of a new friendship, heading into the future.

The ankle Tenzo had hurt was apparently his left, because he tried to stand balancing his weight on his right leg, but when his left foot touched the ground the pain must have shot through him because he whimpered and, turning halfway around, nearly fell back down. I surprised myself by nimbly reaching out to catch him.

"Let's go to the hospital."

"No need for that."

"Why?"

"I don't have a Health Insurance Card."

"Do you have one at home?" Looking troubled, Tenzo moved his lips but said nothing.

"Where do you live?" I asked.

I was getting too close for comfort. Putting a hand up to stop me, begging me with his eyes not to ask anything more, he said, "It's not broken, only sprained, so ice will be enough."

"How can you tell?"

"I spent a long time roaming around places where there weren't any doctors, so I learned to diagnose myself."

Exposed to rain, wind, and sun until it was the texture of fine leather, his skin fitted the word "roaming." But the way his eyes moved, always looking around, suggested a young boy crazy about computers. Perhaps he was Native American or Asian American, born in a city in America, and had run away at the age of fifteen or so, traveled around Alaska or Siberia, and eventually made his way to Germany. My imagination had wandered over such a wide geographical space that I didn't know how to get it back under control. It's a bad habit of mine to start writing in my head the biography of someone I've just met. So here I was, making up a past for this young man when I should have been taking him home to treat his sprained ankle.

To get out of this underground passage we had to climb the stairs. Each step was hard labor, with Tenzo's weight pressing down on my shoulder; I was feeling it in my bones, so it was a great relief to finally reach the top. Though it was chilly enough to need a jacket, I felt heat coming from within the young man's body, covered with only a thin layer of cotton. Cars passed us by, each like a steel block with no one inside. I was planning to flag down a taxi if I saw one, but before I knew it we were standing in front of my apartment building. When we got into the elevator, the moment the steel door closed I felt the irritation and anxiety of a wild animal trapped in a steel box. I had never felt this way before. Perhaps Tenzo felt the same way, for he kept his eyes shut while the elevator clanked its way up to the third floor.

When I unlocked the door, my keys rattling like a talisman, I saw the table at the back wall where it always was. There was a cup stained with lipstick and a plate with breadcrumbs on it. Someone had eaten breakfast there that morning before leaving the apartment. Though it was undoubtedly me, it now seemed like some stranger from the distant past.

I always keep the door to the right of the kitchen open a crack. Even on cloudy days, sunlight seems to pour through the narrow space. There is a sofa for guests in that room, and the wall behind it is lined with the titles of books.

As I use the room to the left of the kitchen as my bedroom, I always keep the door shut tight, to keep out the smell of food. But smells aren't the only problem. If I come across a word I can't get out of my head while I'm reading, and end up taking it into the bedroom with me, it will sometimes flit around the room all night like a mosquito, keeping me awake. For instance, a while ago the name Kamchatka made such a fuss I didn't get to sleep until dawn. That's why I've made the bedroom off limits to all printed matter, even magazines. My bed is king-size, big enough for three people to sleep in. Three have only slept in it once, though. My other room, with the door half-open, is the guest room, with a single sofa bed, a desk, and a stool. Last month a friend who lives in Cologne spent a night in this room. I washed and ironed the sheet, coverlet, and pillowcase she used, folded them neatly, and put them on the chair to wait for my next guest. I have a feeling that by preparing in this way, before

I know who it will be, I am enticing that person to come see me.

Unlike my friends, who look curiously around when they come here for the first time, Tenzo stood in the hall staring vacantly into space, waiting for me to tell him what to do. I spread a sheep's wool blanket out on the sofa. A friend gave it to me last year when I injured my anus; sitting on it dulled the pain. Lending Tenzo my shoulder I helped him into the room, carefully sat him down on the sofa, and had him lie down on his side while I placed his injured left foot on top of the blanket. I was going to bandage his ankle but when I checked my first aid kit, I discovered I was out of bandages.

"I'll buy a bandage at the pharmacy," I said, but shaking his head, Tenzo squirmed and wriggled until he had his T-shirt off, then proceeded to take hold of a frayed seam and rip off a strip of cloth. His movements were smooth, as if he did this sort of thing all the time.

I have a past I've kept hidden from my colleagues at work. My skill with a bandage grew directly out of that past. It was a time when, due to feelings so passionate and rebellious the term adolescence cannot begin to encompass them, I intentionally strayed from the path that was laid out for me. Because I could beat my Gymnasium teachers in intellectual debates, and had read more than almost anyone in my class, everyone assumed I would go on to university. But when the time came to start preparing for graduation exams, I suddenly wanted to see the real world. Going to university seemed childish and boring, a mere extension of my years as a Gymnasium student. I was sure I had already read everything students read at university. Just at that time, I was reading a book in which contemporary society was compared to a multitenant building. The tenants are not bound together by common ideals. While they share a desire to protect the building from fire, the inner sufferings of other tenants mean nothing to them. Nor do they care about equality or human rights. Basic principles the state once held in esteem have broken down, so that even if a neighbor is covered in urine and feces, as long as one's own home doesn't smell, one doesn't interfere. This deterioration in the capacity for empathy is what keeps the multitenant building going. "You can never understand how a toilet feels until you yourself are a toilet," the book said, and reading those words made me want to actually become a toilet, or a guardhouse, or maybe a cafeteria for employees. Having a certain "profession" is an illusion, I thought, because in reality, people are defined by the "place" where they end up. There are various kinds of places: some that smell, others that are peaceful, still others where one suffers constant verbal abuse, places that are freezing cold, and places that offer protection. If I went to university, I would automatically be sent to a place in society where I didn't want to go, to the side that exploits. As my parents were too busy getting divorced to have much time for me, they said nothing about my future. My ideal, for the time being, was to become a true member of the working class. I thought first of baking bread, but all the bakeries in my neighborhood belonged to a national chain. I was feeling disappointed when someone told me about a couple on the outskirts of Trier who baked their own bread. I paid them a visit, only to find them very much out of step with my image of the working class. Having turned the ample inheritance they had received from their parents into flour, they spent their days baking an ideal they called bread. Both had PhDs in philosophy. They had only to pronounce the word *brot* (bread) for it to take on ideological reverberations. And though they themselves were baking bread, they lectured me on the necessity of going to university, making it hard for me to decide where they really stood.

If I couldn't work in a bakery, why not a textile mill or clothing factory, I thought, so I made the rounds of local clothing stores, only to find that almost all clothing's imported from abroad. Just after China stopped exporting altogether, it was rumored that the domestic clothing industry might be revived, but even now almost everything is imported, with only a few clothes made in Germany. Someone told me if I really wanted to sew clothes I should become a designer, but that job didn't fit my image of the working class, either. I was trapped in a dead end of my own making when I happened to meet a childhood friend named Silke on the bus. She said she was now a registered nurse, working in a city hospital. I asked her out to dinner, and as I listened to her talk about her job, it seemed to me that even if I couldn't be a registered nurse, I could at least qualify as a nurse's assistant. Silke, however, didn't think that was such a good idea. With furrowed brow, she told me that since I liked books I should go to university. The work registered nurses and nurse's assistants did was not only physically exhausting and nerve-racking as well, but they often weren't even treated like autonomous human beings capable of making their own decisions. "Make a suggestion about how to improve things at the hospital and you'll be ignored, but when there's a problem you'll be held entirely responsible—it happens all the time," she said. I was in my early twenties then, dying to feel inequality in my bones, so this was exactly what I was looking for. I got my certificate and started working in a hospital. Knowing someone might die because of something I did, my nerves were always on edge. While I was still tingling with warmth from the gratitude of one patient, another would remind me of a mistake I'd made. Young doctors would string me along with praise, then when they'd softened me up, they'd slap me down with a harsh scolding to make it clear who was in charge. After several months I got used to the work, but then another problem arose. When I heard a colleague say, "We just put patients on a conveyor belt and either mend them or sprinkle them with medicine to get a chemical reaction, then when we've done our quota, we write our reports," it pierced me to the heart, and I couldn't sleep at night. A short time later, after feeding a journalist information about the unholy alliance between our hospital and a certain drug company, this same colleague decided to quit the hospital. Another suddenly handed in her resignation one day, saying she'd gotten a scholarship to medical school. Finally realizing that I had no interest in medicine, and was not at all suited to caring for sick people or the aged or children, I quit the hospital, and decided I had no place to go but the university. I majored in political science and philosophy, got a job at a local museum after I graduated, where I soon got accustomed to the work and, forgetting all about my months of toil at the hospital, planned to work there until I retired, after which I would enjoy my years as a pensioner, reading and traveling until my age eventually reached that number called "expected life span." I thought from time to time about having a family, but after I broke up with Klemens, I didn't meet anyone new.

And now I was suddenly being called upon to wrap a bandage, actually a strip of cloth torn from an old, worn-out T-shirt, around the ankle of someone as mysterious as a coyote. Comparing a person with exotic looks to an animal is unforgivably prejudiced of me. But actually, I have great respect for coyotes. This is because I am wrapped in layers of cloth like a mummy, and if you unwind that cloth, you'd find nothing inside but a shriveled corpse.

When I had finished bandaging Tenzo's ankle, I got some ice out of the freezer, put it in a sandwich bag, and cinched its top with a rubber band. Tenzo lay back on the sofa with his eyes closed. Now that I couldn't see his eyes, his eyebrows looked much thicker. His long hair was full and shiny all the way to the ends, but his bare chest was perfectly smooth, without a trace of hair. When I put the ice bag on his ankle he started and opened his eyes. I went to the dresser in my bedroom and got out some casual woolen clothes, which I handed to Tenzo.

"You can wear these," I said. "If you're still cold I can give you a hot water bottle."

"Thanks, but I'm not cold at all. In fact, I'm a little too warm. I forgot to ask you before—what's your name?"

"Nora."

"Like in Ibsen. That was the only play I read at school."

"Strange school. Didn't you read Shakespeare?"

"No, we didn't. I guess it was a cultural thing. Almost all our teachers ignored the British Empire but kept going on about the wonders of Scandinavian culture. Actually, though, right now I'm suffering from something that's not very dramatic."

"Tell me all about it."

"My stomach's been empty for a long time. So long, in fact, that the digestive acids are starting to eat away the lining."

"I'm so sorry. I should have asked. What would you like to eat? There's nothing in the refrigerator, but I can get something delivered. Do you like Sicilian pizza? Balkan grill isn't bad either, but my favorite is sushi."

Tenzo burst out laughing.

"What's so funny?" I asked. "Did I say something strange?"

"No, it's just that I was a chef in a sushi place."

"Really?" So that's where he was from—the land of sushi. The mystery was solved, the cloud of haze that had been hovering around my collar disappeared, and I felt refreshed.

"Were you working in a sushi place in Trier?"

"I just arrived in Trier yesterday—never even been here before. I was in a little town in Denmark at first. Then I went to northern Germany, where I worked in Husum."

"Then the sushi I order won't taste very good to you."

"Don't worry about it. The miso soup they serve in the average sushi bar is awful, but even if the sushi's not so good it doesn't really bother me. I'm doing research on dashi now."

"Dashi. They were saying on TV a while ago that dashi is important for making good soup. But what exactly is it? It's one of those words like umami or satori, so popular right now that you hear them all the time, but I bet there aren't many people who actually know what dashi means."

"It's the flavor that comes from deep sea plants, or dried fish."

"Did you grow up by the sea?"

"You might say that. There are oceans all over the world."

"In Trier it's hard to feel the ocean, but we do have sushi bars. I'll call one."

Humming to myself, I went back to the foyer where my telephone was to call a nearby sushi bar. Surprised at how happy I was to suddenly be given this new role as Tenzo's nurse and provider, I picked up the little Buddha figurine on the table beside the phone and gave him a kiss on the forehead.

The delivery took longer than usual. Tenzo fell asleep, sitting up on the sofa. The ability to fall asleep with a vertical torso is in itself worthy of respect. I remembered my grandfather telling me that Asians can even sleep standing up. Yogis in training sleep standing on one leg under the Bodhi Tree. And I had heard something once about people sleeping standing up in crowded trains—wasn't that in the land of sushi? I was still a child then, and it impressed me so much I started practicing to see if I could do it myself. I'd get into bed at night and turn off the light so my mother wouldn't worry, then get up after a while to stand in the dark, trying to sleep. But just the thought of myself standing there in the dark got me so excited I'd be wide awake again. After a while I'd lose my balance and fall on the floor with a great thud, and when my mother came running I had a hard time explaining what I was doing on the floor.

When the doorbell rang Tenzo awoke with a start and opened his eyes. "You took your time," I griped to the delivery boy, but with a big smile and a tip to match. Tenzo must have been awfully hungry, because he pulled the disposable wooden chopsticks apart and started eating right away, not even waiting for me to make tea. He used only a tiny bit of soy sauce, completely ignoring the ginger and wasabi.

"This gari is terrible," Tenzo said, his voice full of contempt as he pointed at the ginger with his chopsticks. "It's full of chemicals." Though the ginger is usually what I start with, picking up as much as I can get between my chopsticks, hearing Tenzo say that dampened my appetite for it. "This 'sabi is just as bad. Looks like green toothpaste kids would go crazy over, don't you think?"

I always dissolve lots of wasabi in the soy sauce and soak the sushi in it before I eat, but I gave up on that too. Eating with a sushi chef made me so nervous I lost my sense of taste.

"Are you sure you don't need to go to hospital?"

"My ankle's already much better."

"Where were you yesterday?"

"I was walking. All the way from Husum."

"That's too far to walk."

"Of course I didn't walk all that way in a day. I got a ride partway."

"Do you have money?"

"Enough to live for a while."

"Don't you have any luggage?"

"I did but it was stolen the day before yesterday. It was just a rucksack, though, and there wasn't anything valuable in it."

"What are you going to do now?"

"Find a job."

"You can stay here until you can walk."

Maybe he was used to hearing that sort of thing because without seeming surprised or hesitant about accepting my offer, he just quietly thanked me.

From that day on, our life together began. Eager to find out about his childhood, I'd ask him leading questions.

"What did you like to do when you were a child?"

"Mmm, playing outside maybe."

"What games did you play? Sumo? Baseball?"

"I liked animals, so I spent a lot of time watching them."

"Were there lots of animals around? I guess you weren't raised in a big city then. Where did you live?"

"Kumamoto," he mumbled, then looked as if he regretted saying it.

"Is that in the north, or the south?"

"South. But after a big explosion in a factory nearby no one could live there anymore, so we moved up north."

"Where in the north?"

He sat there blinking, looking confused for a while but then he finally came out with "Karafuto," as if he'd just thought of it.

"That's a place I've never heard of."

As if telling me he wanted to end the conversation there, he got up and left, saying he was going to look for a job.

Several places served sushi in Trier, but most specialized in either Thai curry or Vietnamese food, with sushi as a side attraction. If you included Tapas and Sushi, which was run by Spaniards, and the Seven Seas, a place that served fish dishes from around the world, there were actually quite a few possibilities, but apparently none of them wanted to hire Tenzo. He seemed so disappointed I felt sorry for him, but then I had an idea. A pretty wild idea, the kind that an amateur like me would come up with, but I still thought it was worth a try. The city had started a new campaign, asking ordinary people to submit ideas for small festivals. Trier isn't a very large city, and as these were to be neighborhood festivals, any proposal had a fair chance of being accepted. I had just seen a program on TV about dashi and umami, so I knew there was a growing interest. What if Tenzo were to give a lecture and demonstration? He didn't seem very enthusiastic at first, but when after another week he still hadn't found a job, he half-heartedly agreed. I immediately started filling out the application form.

"I have to write your full name on this form."

"It's Tenzo."

"Is that your family name, or your given name?"

"Both. Didn't you know? A long time ago there were a violinist called Midori and a baseball player named Ichiro. People where I'm from sometimes have just one name."

I wrote a rather vague proposal but it was accepted anyway, and after I got funding from the city, my plan for the festival began to take shape. At the main event, the chef instructor would stand on a platform and explain exactly what dashi and umami were as he actually was making dashi from seaweed and dried fish in a pan on a hotplate. He would then use the dashi to prepare a few simple dishes. The audience would be able to taste what he had made and ask questions. I would recruit another chef instructor to demonstrate making dashi for Italian food, plus a budding nutritionist to complete the program. The head of the museum, though reluctant at first, agreed to lend us the space. I printed the posters myself, and went around to restaurants and libraries asking people to put them up.

But when the preparations were completed, just five days before the festival was to be held, Tenzo suddenly announced that he was going to Norway. He said there was to be a public dinner in Oslo, a competition for a few carefully selected chefs. It was an open secret that the real purpose of the dinner was to choose the preparation committee for the Nobel Prize dinner, so he couldn't refuse.

"I'll be back in Trier in time for the event, though," he said coolly. "I'll decide what to do afterward then." He showed me his airline ticket. He'd be leaving on the evening of that day, and had a return flight reserved for the morning of the festival.

It wasn't that I didn't believe Tenzo. I was disconcerted, though, at how much this news upset me. Though I was used to being alone, during the short time I'd lived with Tenzo I'd gotten even more used to having another body around: *Used to* doesn't sound so heavy, but when what you're used to is about to be ripped away you notice that a tree of emotion has grown inside you. I was certain that Tenzo had feelings for me, too. They reminded me of a black river flowing slowly, heavily, through a snowy field, splitting it in two. At night that river flowed straight toward me, growing warmer, giving rise to a strong wind that extinguished my consciousness like a candle flame. The next morning I would have no memory of what had happened next. No image whatsoever. All I could think of were scenes I had seen of people having sex in the movies. When I tried to reproduce what we had done in my head, all I saw was a droll dance of verbs like thrust, suck, lick, squeeze, entangle, or shake, with neither subjects nor objects. Because I had no memories I could record and reproduce, I had to repeat the sex act every night. Tenzo said nothing about it, and didn't leave even the tiniest opening for me to mention it, either. Klemens, the guy I'd been with before, took great pleasure in putting even the smallest details into words. He'd calmly go on about how the upward curve of excitement just before ejaculation had been too sharp, or how he'd rather I didn't shave my legs so often, or about how he found it more stimulating when I sat on top of him with my blouse still buttoned. With Tenzo I had entered a world without words — there was nothing to hold onto. Though I didn't feel particularly uneasy there, it was like living day by day, with no idea of what tomorrow would bring. Like being in the middle of a snowy wasteland with no shops around and no food stored up. Since I didn't have a contract I could show him to make him stay, if Tenzo suddenly vanished I would be left with nothing. Tenzo had given me no words, not "lover," or even "relationship."

Though I had planned to see him off at the airport, during the half hour while I was out shopping, Tenzo disappeared. He didn't even leave a note. If I were to tell someone that for a short time a man called Tenzo had been living with me, I would surely be told I'd been dreaming. He was so shy that whenever I offered to introduce him to my friends, or take him to meet the head of the museum, he always shook his head no. So not a single person around me even knew of his existence.

He'd promised to let me know when he got to Oslo, but I didn't hear from him the next day or the day after that. Finally he called me on the morning the festival was to be held.

When I'd finished taping my cancellation notice to the museum door, the pensioner was waiting to continue our conversation, but I gave him my phone number and said goodbye. I had stickers with the word *Canceled* to put on the posters I'd distributed around the neighborhood. Even if I couldn't catch them all, I had to do what I could. I first went to a nearby sushi bar, only to find that the poster had already been torn off, with just bits of paper left around the tacks. At the Irish pub, a notice for a Catholic Rock Concert had been pasted over mine, so you could hardly read it. The only poster that was still up and clearly visible was the one at the city library. I was angry, yet relieved at the same time. It didn't matter how many *Canceled* stickers I managed to post, since hardly anyone would know about it anyway. Perhaps from relief, I suddenly felt hungry, so I bought a kebab sandwich and headed for the Kaiserthermen. Ancient Rome was now not only a place I loved, but a place full of memories, where I had first met Tenzo. I sat down on a stone in the grassy field in the midst of the ruins and bit into the bread, first on the right side, then on the left. I was eating exactly like the pet dog I used to have. Thinking about her made me want another dog. After I finished my sandwich I went down into the underground passageway, longing to visit the spot where I had found Tenzo. I thought I was alone when I saw three human figures up ahead, coming toward me. With the sun at my back, I could see their faces clearly, though probably all they could see of me was a dark shadow. One was a man with blond hair, another a woman whose face resembled Tenzo's, and the third, whose face looked like a man's although he was dressed like a woman, seemed to be Indian. All three looked a little frightened for some reason, so to put them at ease, I called out, "Hello." I was quite sure they hadn't taken me for an ancient Roman ghost, though. When we were about a yard apart, we all stopped walking.

"Are you here sightseeing?" I asked the blond man in German, but to my surprise it was not he but the Indian man next to him who answered, in fluent German.

"I live in Trier," he said, "but these two have come from Denmark. Sightseeing? No, not really."

"So they're not tourists?"

"Well, they certainly didn't come to see ancient Roman ruins. Actually, there's an event at the Karl Marx House today, and they left Denmark this morning to be in time for it."

Astonished, I stood there frowning, not knowing what to say until the Indian, as if to calm me down, added in a gentle voice, "My name is Akash."

The blond man, who although he didn't speak German apparently understood it, put out his hand and introduced himself in English, "My name's Knut." The woman who bore some resemblance to Tenzo then bowed slightly and said, in a barely audible voice, "Hiruko," which perhaps was her name. Still somewhat depressed, I decided to cheer myself up by explaining the situation in English.

"My name is Nora. I work at the Karl Marx House. I was supposed to be in charge of the event you came to see. But as Tenzo, the chef instructor, was unable to return from Oslo this morning, I've had to cancel the event, which is a big problem for me."

Despite their extreme physical differences, Knut and Hiruko gasped in exactly the same way.

"And why is Meister Tenzo unable to come back from Oslo?" Akash asked, knitting his brow.

"The political situation is in turmoil, and all international flights have been canceled."

"Norway? In political turmoil?" barked Knut, repeating what I had said. Unlike the pensioner from that morning, he threw my words straight back at me. This pierced me to the heart. Norway *couldn't* be in political turmoil. Tenzo must have lied to escape from me. Why hadn't he told me the truth? Akash took his Smilephone out of his pocket, but the ruins were apparently blocking reception.

"Let's go outside."

We hurried back to the main road and found a coffee shop. Akash furiously hunted for information on his Smilephone, and after a while, said in English, "It seems there is something bad going on in Oslo. A terrorist attack." This was a big relief. Tenzo hadn't deceived me after all. "But international flights are apparently departing on schedule," Akash added, his fingers still darting across the screen in search of more information.

I had an idea of what the problem might be, though I didn't say it out loud. Even if international flights were leaving on schedule, with border surveillance tightened due to the terrorist attack, perhaps Tenzo had been stopped at the border. Though he never told me about it in detail, there seemed to be some problem with his residence status or passport. Although normally he would be able to travel freely through Europe, when there was a terrorist incident he would have trouble crossing borders. Perhaps that was why he wasn't able to return to Trier. At this point Hiruko, who had been virtually silent until then, suddenly said in English, "Tenzo probably doesn't have a passport. Our country has now disappeared. So valid passports no longer exist. Usually we can travel through Europe without showing a passport, but when there is terrorism, you can't even go into the airport without showing identification."

My whole body shivering, I suddenly blurted out "I am going to Oslo."

"I'll go too," Hiruko immediately chimed in.

"Pardon me for asking," I said, not wanting to miss this chance, "but are you related to Tenzo?"

"No. I haven't met him yet, but I think we are in similar situation. That's why I want to meet him."

Knut was more practical. "I'll go too," he said, "but first I've got to go back to Copenhagen and apply for a leave of absence. I'm attached to an office in the linguistics department, so there's no problem if I take a few days off, but if I don't do the paperwork someone's bound to complain. So I won't be able to fly to Oslo today, but I can probably make it back tomorrow or the next day." He sounded as if he were Hiruko's partner.

"I also have to go back to Odense to get official permission to take time off work," said Hiruko. "Usually they don't give it on such short notice, but I have much overtime so I think I can manage. I'll return to Odense, and if possible, fly to Oslo tomorrow."

"I can't go," said Akash, looking terribly sad. "Traveling to Oslo is much too expensive for a student. But I hope you will keep in touch, and tell me what's happening."

"I'll come back to Trier as soon as I can," I said, feeling sorry for him. "You can call me any time, and I'll tell you how things are in Oslo." I hoped this would comfort him, but to tell the truth, I couldn't understand why not being able to go to Oslo should make him so sad. I could see why Hiruko wanted to meet Tenzo, because they were from the same country. And Knut liked Hiruko, so it was natural for him to want to go with her, but what sort of relationship did Akash have with these two?

"Do you know where in Oslo Tenzo is?" Knut asked coolly.

"He said there was some kind of contest, to be held at a restaurant called Nise-Fuji," I said, and Hiruko, whose face had been a mask of sadness until then, suddenly burst out laughing as if she'd never heard anything so funny. Knut and Akash both gave her puzzled looks.

"Nise-Fuji means Fake Mt. Fuji," Hiruko finally managed to

explain when she got her laughter under control. Suddenly I felt embarrassed.

"When I got the telephone call, there was interference, as if a strong wind were blowing, so I couldn't hear Tenzo very well," I said by way of an excuse. "He might have said 'Shinise-Fuji' rather than 'Nise-Fuji.'"

"I like Nise-Fuji much better," said Hiruko, still looking happy, and grateful for this funny word that had brought her laughter back.

"When we will meet again?" asked Akash, sounding sentimental as he gazed longingly at Knut.

"We're all living on a huge ball," replied Knut, placing a big hand on Akash's slender shoulder. "No place is very far away. We can meet anytime, as many times as we like. Akash, you stay in Trier and wait for Tenzo to come back. We'll each fly to Oslo on our own, and, hopefully, meet up in the afternoon or evening of the day after tomorrow at the Nise-Fuji."

Nora got me all wrong. And I didn't even try to set her right.

I started pretending to be from the land of sushi long before I met her. True, outside forces lured me into it, but as I kept working on my act, looking up stuff I had to know to perfect it, I made it into a work of art.

The country where I was born and brought up is nothing like the land of sushi. They had a population explosion, and after that there were so many people in the cities that even with trains coming every few minutes they couldn't fit everybody in. I can still remember how excited the announcer I saw once on a Danish TV show sounded, going on about how men used to be paid just to push passengers' backs to squeeze them into the trains. To a kid like me that was like something out of a fairy tale. The trains were so packed that there'd be people pressing up against you on all sides, so many that you could sleep standing up. They called that *sushi-zume,* packed in like pieces of sushi in a box. That was the land of sushi all right. How I envied them.

The fishing village in Greenland where I grew up was just the opposite. Our population started out small and kept getting smaller until finally the village primary school nearly had to close. Just when I was looking forward to starting school, families with kids my age moved away one after the other until I was the only new pupil left. Seven had graduated the year before, but that was just a fluke. If things went on this way, the school would close for sure. And then the whole village would shut down. Looking troubled, the adults got together and decided to write a letter to the Danish government. Luckily, that year the government had just increased its budget for aid to the arctic territories, so they made a rule saying "No primary school will be closed, no matter how small the enrollment," and on top of that, sent dozens of families from Copenhagen to be our new neighbors.

"What sort of people," the grown-ups asked, looking troubled again, "would want to move to Greenland from the capital of Denmark? Fine if they're tired of city life and want to live quietly, surrounded by nature, but what if they're ex-cons?" Though Denmark has a low crime rate, there was one crime that was on the rise. That was hate speech. We sure didn't want a bunch of people who hated and might even attack nonwhites coming to our village. I was still little, but I used to toss and turn in bed at night, with waves of hope first, and then anxiety, washing over me, keeping me from falling into a nice, deep pocket of sleep.

The new people who moved to our village were not Danish. They had dark hair, deeply honed features, and eyes so big they couldn't possibly have opened them any wider. The men had beards, and the women covered their heads with scarves. I heard much later that to escape from war they had come all the way from North Africa, but because there weren't enough houses for them in the city, the government promised them living expenses and subsidies if they would move to Greenland. They arrived in summer, but our summers, like hope, don't last very long: they are followed by endless winters. The children learned Greenlandic as they played, and soon got used to the cold. Forgetting their ingrained fear and hatred of dogs, they happily played with them, too. The grown-ups, on the other hand, shut themselves indoors from morning to night, occasionally opening the door halfway to peer fearfully out at the snow and the dogs. Since they were living on government funds they didn't have to go out to work, and being suddenly left with nothing to do must have been hard for them.

Of course, immigrants weren't the only ones without jobs. My parents had spent their whole lives there, but when they were young, they couldn't find work either. The fish stocks had thinned out, which put an end to fishing. The sea otters were almost gone, and when somebody managed to bag a seal, it got on the evening news. It was getting warmer, and farming became possible, and Ma was one of the first to start planting potatoes and cabbages in the garden, her harvest growing year by year. Pa never got used to the taste of vegetables, though. He ordered Danish canned ham and sausages on the internet, which meant he needed more cash coming in. So he brushed up on his English and got a job with an American company. Not that he moved to America or anything. He worked from home, answering customers' questions on the telephone. When some lady in an American town called the company with a complaint about the vacuum cleaner she'd bought, it was Pa who picked up the receiver.

"I want to throw away the bag where the dirt collects but I can't find it."

I remember a time when Pa got lots of complaints like that. It said in the user's manual that this new type of vacuum cleaner didn't have a bag inside, but I guess most people didn't bother to read it. The dirt sucked up in these newfangled vacuum cleaners disappeared naturally after it was burned at a low temperature. The bits of ash that were left over formed into a ball. It took ten years for that ball of ash to get big enough so you'd have to throw it away. But as Pa patiently explained, with new models coming out all the time, there was no way anyone was still going to be using the same vacuum cleaner ten years later.

He sounded really funny to me, carefully answering all these questions about the latest model of a vacuum cleaner he had never seen. That's how I learned English—by ear. Even Pa got mad sometimes when people asked him the same question over and over again. He'd get sarcastic and say things like, "It would be quicker if you'd just read the user's manual."

"But a computer must have written it," the customer would whine, "and I hate reading stuff like that. I mean, the sentences are so awful—guess you'd call it robot prose. You sound completely different. Just listening to you speak real English makes me feel alive," which put Pa in a really good mood, ready to chat as long as the customer wanted. There were people who couldn't have cared less about their vacuum cleaner, but just called because they were lonely and wanted to talk. One woman phoned every week, and always asked for Pa. Once when, just to tease him, I told him he was her "call boy," he got really mad.

The company in America was always watching him, making sure he kept the telephone connected, and checking how satisfied his customers were. Since he was under contract to work sixteen hours a day, he always kept his headset on, at meals and even when he was on the toilet taking a dump. Maybe that's why that vacuum cleaner sometimes seems like a younger brother I grew up with.

Ma, on the other hand, got a job with a wellness center deep in the Swiss mountains. She kept records of each patient's blood pressure and calorie intake, which she analyzed and used to work out daily schedules for them, sending messages like, "In ten minutes it will be eight o'clock. Are you ready to go jogging?" to make sure they kept to the plan. Whenever she got an answer like, "I don't feel like doing anything today," she had to think up a catchy phrase to urge her patient on. If she used the same one all the time they'd think she was a computer program, so she was always changing the wording, slipping in misspelled words now and then to make her messages seem more human. But becoming friends with clients on an individual basis was strictly forbidden.

Thanks to these jobs, money kept coming into our bank account every month, and I grew up free of hardship. I could get whatever I wanted—canned pineapple, a hamster, or a soccer ball—just by ordering it on the internet. We could stay this way for several generations, never leaving home, connected to the global economy only through the internet ... or could we? What if the things we saw on the computer screen were just what somebody had cooked up, and the outside world no longer existed? True, whatever we ordered came right on time. But what if there was only one huge factory somewhere across the sea where everything we ordered was manufactured, and the rest of the world had disappeared?

When I went out for a walk after sunset, I'd listen to the dogs howling in the distance until my heart ached with a longing for faraway places. I wanted to travel. The only faraway place I could imagine myself in at that point was Reykjavik, the capital of Iceland. I could see myself walking between rows of neat little houses there, but I wanted to go farther, maybe all the way to Denmark. And spread out south of Denmark was a country called Germany. Although it was much smaller than Greenland, in Germany there were lots of different cultures: in the north, descendants of the Vikings; to the south, ruins of the Roman Empire; in the east, Slavic smells that filled the air.

One day when I was looking at a map of the world, lost in thought, Pa came along looking very serious and said, "Nanook, get yourself a scholarship and go study at a university in Copenhagen." That's my name—Nanook. There were lots of different scholarships, and I'd heard it wasn't too hard to get one.

Ma wasn't as enthusiastic as Pa was about the idea of my studying abroad. Lots of young people went to study in Denmark and didn't come back.

"When we get old, we'll be lonely without our son nearby," she grumbled, but Pa scolded her. "How can you cling to him like that?" he said. "Besides, if he stays here, he'll end up doing the same kind of work we do, but in the outside world, he can do anything." His eyes growing brighter, he added, "Just imagine our son as head of the Kingdom Hospital in Copenhagen!" Actually, he only knew about that hospital from a drama he'd seen on TV—he'd never been to Copenhagen. And on that TV show, the hospital didn't exactly come off as a respectable medical institution; in fact, it was an awful place, where the doctors, who thought only of getting ahead, sacrificed their patients to power struggles, and once in a while the ghost of a dead patient would appear in the elevator. Pa must have forgotten about all that stuff. If not, he never would have wanted me to become the head of a hospital like that, full of ghosts. If he'd wanted me to be a shaman, to calm those angry spirits, I'd understand, but Pa was a half-hearted Christian with a blind faith in modern medicine, probably because he'd never been to the doctor.

I didn't like television very much, but I never missed a single rerun of that old drama *The Kingdom* that Pa used to watch. It was directed by someone called Lars von Trier. At the end of every episode, he would come on looking like a mischievous kid and ask, "How did you like that?" Maybe that's why Trier, the name of a German city, sounds friendly to me even now. It seems Lars von Trier's family moved north from there, which is why they have that surname.

After getting my high school diploma by correspondence, I decided to study in Copenhagen. Since I'd missed the deadline for government scholarships, I applied to a charitable foundation run by one person. Right away a letter came back from a woman named Inga Nielsen, telling me she'd pay for my tuition and living expenses. I wrote and told her that I first wanted to study at a language school to improve my Danish language skills, and then study natural science at university. I didn't want to study medicine and end up working in a hospital full of ghosts, but Greenland needed doctors, and I had heard it was easier to study abroad if you said you wanted to study medicine. So though I didn't really mean to trick Mrs. Nielsen, in my letter I wrote "(medicine, for instance)" after "natural science." I was more interested in zoology, because I wanted to spend my days watching sea otters, polar bears, and whales when I came back to Greenland.

"If you get lonely, come right home," a friend told me, looking troubled just like the grown-ups. I had no idea what loneliness was yet, so I wasn't worried. "I envy you, going to such a warm place," one of the girls said. To us, Denmark is practically the tropics. Though it's pretty far north, the warm sea currents keep it from getting much snow, so winters there don't last for months on end.

There were no direct flights to Copenhagen, so I had to fly to Reykjavik first, but then there were no flights until spring. Rich tourists or politicians probably hire charter flights, but I'd bought a discount ticket with Pa's credit card. I registered for language school online, and got a room in a dorm. After throwing some clean clothes and my dictionary into a sports bag, I put my passport and wallet into my jacket pocket.

A cloudy sky hung over the airport like the lid of a huge aluminum pan. As if it were being lowered down over my memories, and when it covered them completely, then I would be sucked into the big body of the airplane in front of me. People think that airplanes are just machines, metal plates and screws put together by human hands, but didn't this beautiful shape come from the spirits of birds playing with human beings, guiding them to make airplanes in their own image? Of course human beings believe they invented a machine with the best shape for flying, by their own will. But maybe an airplane is really a mythical bird, come to save us. Ma gave me a cross as an amulet. Pa mumbled, "Take care of yourself," in a voice that sounded very quiet for him.

What surprised me most in Copenhagen was that, while everything I saw there surprised me, no one seemed surprised to see me. Passersby never stared at me, and there were no kids pointing, yelling, "Look, there's an Eskimo!"

I thought there would be lots of cars, but I didn't see any in the center of Copenhagen. Instead there were bicycles, speeding through the streets. All the people I saw lightly swinging their legs to get off their bikes in front of bookstores or coffee shops were really skinny. I was sure there would be lots of shops in the city selling sweets and slabs of meat that made everybody fat, but the signs in all the shop windows said "Sugar-free" or "Vegetarian." And I couldn't believe how low the prices were. When I saw the price of the hot dogs some guy was selling from a cart attached to his bicycle, I was shocked. Remembering how much we used to pay for canned sausages, I started to wonder if that canned goods company wasn't playing us for suckers.

And one more thing. In this country, hot drinks never cooled down no matter how long you waited. I went into a coffee shop with a big glass window so you could see everything inside, and ordered something called café soy latte. The liquid hidden under the layer of white foam on top was hot enough to burn your tongue. A memory came back. It was something that happened before I started primary school. One day when Grandpa took me fishing, he brushed away the snow and made a hole in the ice so we could see the dark sea beneath. The water was much warmer than the air outside. But that day we only caught one fish. I was still little, but even now I remember thinking that our life as fishermen was just about over.

I don't like hot drinks, so I waited a long time before putting my lips to the cup again, but the coffee underneath the foam had hardly cooled off at all. Nothing to do but wait some more, so I stared through the window at the street outside until I heard a voice say, "Do you mind if I sit here?" I looked up into the eyes of a blonde girl about my age. Without waiting for me to answer, she filled the empty space beside me with the smell of roses. "What're you drinking? Café soy latte?" she asked. "You really should try Classic Cappuccino. It's much better. My name is Anna. Is today Tuesday or Wednesday? Anyway, about that election we just had ..." She forged ahead, talking at full speed, switching topics like she was jumping from one ice floe to the next. I could hardly keep up with her. She probably knew right away that Danish wasn't my native tongue, but didn't bother to ask where I was from. From the look on her face, she seemed to think anyone could tell at a glance.

Because she was a university student, Anna decided I must be one, too. That made me feel kind of good. "My seminar in Buddhist terminology was canceled today," she said as casually as if I were family. I was nervous at first: there are swindlers in the city so be wary when a stranger talks to you, I had been told. But I soon relaxed. Anna's eyes were a magic mirror; reflected in them, I was starting to look like a charming young man I had never met. I was having a really good time.

When I told her I hadn't started university classes yet, but was still going to language school, she didn't seem disappointed. "I'm in a Classic Manga Research Circle," she said, "and my dream is to one day read Osamu Tezuka's *Buddha* in the original. Would you tandem with me? Where are you living now? Oh! I have to go. I'll be late for class. Call me sometime, okay?" She scrawled her phone number on a scrap of paper and handed it to me. *Tandem* sounded like some secret Buddhist sect devoted to sex, so I got nervous again and didn't call her. Much later I found out that tandem meant two people teaching each other their native languages, but I had never heard of Osamu what's-his-name, and couldn't see why she wanted to learn Greenlandic.

I got nervous again the first time I went to see Mrs. Nielsen, the lady paying for my tuition and living expenses; in fact, I was so stiff I had trouble climbing the stairs. I had never gone to visit someone I didn't know before, or been inside the home of a woman who lived alone. At first I thought she was probably a widow, but I didn't see any pictures that looked like a husband. Maybe she was divorced. On the dresser there was a picture of a cute little boy. She told me it was her son at the age of five, though he was all grown up now, studying linguistics. He had blond curly hair, round cheeks, and eyes so blue the color almost spilled out of them.

After that, I went to visit Mrs. Nielsen several times. I'd ring the bell, pull open the heavy outside door, and climb the stairs to the third floor, smelling all kinds of fragrances as I went, although I smelled only one when I was standing in front of Mrs. Nielsen's door. Then I'd push open another heavy door, close it behind me, and go to the living room at the back of the apartment. Mrs. Nielsen was always standing by the window, holding onto the curtain as if that was all she had, looking down, her profile dark and gloomy. When I said, "Hello," from the doorway, she turned around, her face lighting up like flowers in bloom as soon as she saw me. Strangely enough, I always noticed the oranges and yellows in the bouquet on the dresser just at that moment.

One time Mrs. Nielsen asked, "Are you planning to study medicine at university?" Without thinking, I nodded. The next time, while we were having tea, she got a phone call from someone who, judging from the tone of her voice, must have been very close to her. She was telling whoever it was that I was studying medicine. This won't do, I thought, so as soon as she hung up I said, "I'm still going to language school, and haven't chosen my major yet. Even if I want to study medicine, I don't know if I'll be able to," but she just smiled and said, "All your wishes will come true."

To tell the truth, I never wanted to study medicine. At the time, I was getting interested in environmental biology as a major. I found out about this area of study from George, an American I'd met at the language school.

"Are you from Greenland?" he'd asked me one day after class, and when I nodded, he grinned and said, "Let's be friends." George told me he had grown up on the West Coast. When I asked him why he'd come to Denmark, he said, "I'm sick of living in a Great Power, and wanted to try a little country." I guess Americans think of their country as Great, which must mean big. Other people's heads are full of the strangest thoughts. Coming out this way in a conversation, they can really surprise you.

Greenland is about fifty times the size of Denmark, but when I came to Copenhagen, I didn't feel like I was in a "little country." For starters, I hadn't really grasped "country" as a concept yet, so when people asked me where I was from I used to say "the Arctic Circle," which got me a lot of strange looks.

I learned lots of things from George. He was the one who taught me the word "postcolonialism." And he told me that lots of people who consider the word "Eskimo" racist think it's enough just to replace it with "Inuit," even though strictly speaking not all Eskimos are Inuit. Just as not all gypsies are Roma.

A long time ago, "Eskimo" was generally believed to mean "those who eat raw fish," which sounded terrible to most people. In time, linguists started saying it actually meant "those who tie on snow shoes." That sounds kind of poetic. It must be hard for Asian people to imagine snowshoes made out of reindeer hide, though, because I've heard they take "Eskimo" to mean "those who weave snowshoes from straw"—that makes them feel like they have some kind of bond with us, even though there's no straw where we live.

But anyway, I can't see what's wrong with "those who eat raw fish." To me, eating fish or meat raw when it's fresh seems much more civilized than boiling your food until it turns to mush.

Just once, George and I had an argument. It started with him saying, "Traditional Eskimo hunting culture is under threat from global warming." As if suddenly possessed by Ma's living spirit, I said, "But thanks to global warming now we can grow vegetables. There's no need to stick to the old ways." That surprised George, who came back with, "But wasn't hunting the mainstay of your traditional culture? And aren't you losing it because of climate change and pressure from animal rights activists?" This time I was possessed by Pa's living spirit. "We Eskimos never hunted because we liked it; we killed only as many animals as we needed to live, then preserved the meat and ate it slowly, never wasting it, and used the skins to make our clothes and shoes," I explained. "Then foreign fur traders came to trick us, threatening us until soon we were killing as many sea otters as we could because their fur could be sold at high prices. After many years there were no more sea otters nearby, so we started making long trips in search of new hunting grounds. But that time was like a bad dream we don't want to remember. Now that it's over, we are all relieved." When Pa told me that story it was so boring I only listened with one ear, so it was strange how it all came back to me now, word for word. And what's more, I'd said "we," like I was setting myself up as the representative of my people. George was shocked. "I see now," he said, admitting defeat. "What you say is really deep."

George worshipped Eskimo culture. He was always saying that no other culture had crossed so many borders to spread over such a wide area—Canada, Alaska, Russia, Greenland.

And since Eskimo civilization grew naturally out of ice and snow, they had no need to carve out an artificial "love for the fatherland"; they didn't have to treat anyone who criticized their society like a traitor or get everyone to rally around the flag. By contrast, George said, his own country was based on competition and greed, and because everybody thought only of themselves, the whole society was always in danger of falling apart. It was left to the politicians, with their public speaking skills and charisma, to somehow hold the country together.

I had no reason to criticize some country across the sea I knew nothing about, and while I wasn't especially proud of being an Eskimo — unlike George, I had no romantic illusions about Eskimo culture — I didn't feel inferior, either. But all the same, living in Copenhagen, I was driven into a sort of ethnic corner. The minute they saw me, people put me into a certain category. If you were to give that category a name, it wouldn't be "Asian," or "Muslim," or "person of color," or "immigrant" but definitely Eskimo. When I bought a hot dog at a stand, the man would look surprised as he gave me my change, as if he was thinking "You Eskimos eat sausages?" At the barbershop I'd point to a photo in the catalogue and say, "This is the style I want," only to hear the scissors whisper, "Didn't know you people liked anime-inspired hairstyles." I'd order a drink at a club and see in the bartender's eyes, "Your Eskimo liver doesn't have the enzymes to break down alcohol. Drink this and you'll pass out." It would have been easier if they'd just called out, "Hey you, Eskimo!" but nobody did. Though they weren't cruel, they must have thought it was best not to have much to do with me, because they never looked me in the eye. I felt like my body was wrapped in cellophane stamped with the word *Eskimo* on it — when people saw me, their eyes stopped on the surface, and never went any deeper.

George went back to America before he'd finished his language-school course. "Danish pronunciation is just too difficult," he said, "No matter how hard I work at it I'll never get any better. There's no use trying anymore." But if people all over the world had given up studying English because it's hard to pronounce, English wouldn't have spread so far and wide. George should have tried a little harder.

After George left I had no one to talk to. I wanted a friend. People talked to me often enough, but unfortunately they were all girls with lips as red as cowberries, which they'd bring right up close, blowing their sweet breath in my face as they spoke. I seemed to be popular with girls. As their eyes caressed me, my appearance changed. I grew my hair long enough to cover my ears, and carefully shaved my beard and eyebrows. My eyelashes are long and thick, to protect my eyes from the arctic cold. Having pale skin seems to bother Danish guys, so some of them lie down stark naked in a machine like a huge toaster to burn themselves once a week, but my skin's always been a mixture of gold, brown, and pink. Every morning, I stood in front of the mirror, trying to look like the hero of my favorite anime.

Though it was fun being popular with girls, dating them was scary. I had heard that almost all Danish women have their own income, because they get jobs after they graduate. The gap between rich and poor is so small for both men and women that there aren't very many influential or powerful people, either. So women don't choose a man for his wealth or rank in society. In fact, they hate arrogant men, or men who think too much about getting ahead and making money. What they really want is a kind man who likes children, and when they get hold of him, they try to get pregnant as soon as possible. What scared me most was getting a woman pregnant and not being able to go home to Greenland.

I finally made friends with a guy named Jorn—he was studying anthropology but wanted to be a film director someday. I could talk to him about anything, so one day I told him why dating Danish girls scared me. He just laughed and said, "No Danish girl's going to force you to marry her just because she's pregnant. Some people even say that single mothers are the only upper class left in our classless society, though they used to have a hard time of it."

"But I'd hate to leave my child with its mother here and go back to Greenland by myself," I said. "I want my whole family to live together in Greenland. So what worries me is whether a Danish woman would be willing to come to Greenland."

Jorn looked really surprised. "Why do you need to live in the same place?" he asked. "When I was in kindergarten my mother started a company in Los Angeles and my father was working in Hong Kong, but they never got divorced, so I went back and forth between the two places by plane every two weeks. I picked a university that wasn't in either place, but right here in Copenhagen. Though both my parents are Swedish, I'm the only one living in Scandinavia now. And no matter how busy they are, they always come to Copenhagen for Christmas. Greenland's not so far away. You could go every week if you wanted."

As I listened to Jorn, the map in my head started to change. I now saw that, depending on how you looked at the world, faraway places may not be so far away after all. And though I'd always thought of that small fishing village as home, maybe now I could call all of Greenland and Scandinavia my home, too

Though I didn't particularly miss my village, sometimes I'd suddenly get homesick for the taste of certain foods. I missed flavors of the sea, and of the creatures that live in it. At home we usually ate canned sausages and ham, but several times a month Ma would get some seal meat out of the freezer for Pa and me to defrost and eat. When somebody caught a fish now and them, we'd have that, too, though we usually ordered farm-raised salmon over the internet. Maybe women are better at adapting to the changing times; after a while Ma hardly ate any meat at all, just kept farming more and more land, growing not only cabbage and potatoes, but even lettuce and tomatoes for the salads she started making.

Once I was talking to Anira, an Indian girl I'd gotten to know at the language school, about how I missed the flavors of the sea, and she told me about a place called Samurai where you could eat raw fish. She said lunch was pretty cheap there, so I went one day at about one o'clock in the afternoon. It was crowded, with people lined up at the door. I waited ten minutes or so before I was shown to a table for two, and ordered "Lunch Set Number Five." I was just sitting there, staring into space when a young woman who was wearing a business suit but looked more like a student asked if I'd mind if she sat across from me. I don't much like looking into a stranger's face while I eat, but—thinking how sad I'd be if someone refused me a seat in a crowded restaurant—I couldn't say no.

After my order came, the woman watched me carefully, staring at my hands, though she smiled when our eyes met. Fortunately I'd learned how to use chopsticks by then, but if there were rules about how to eat this stuff, I was sure I was breaking all of them. "When you prepare fish as sashimi, isn't the direction you cut it in really important?" she asked in Danish. Though her accent was a little strange, she sounded certain that I'd know the answer to her question. But what was this sashimi she was talking about? I'd thought this dish was called sushi, but I must have been wrong. I'd just ordered by number, pointing at a picture on the menu, so I didn't really remember. Luckily, just then something Grandpa had once said came back to me: "Cutting salmon is easy if you know just the right angle to place the knife." As most of the salmon I ate was farm-raised fillets, this memory was buried under a thick layer of ice, but somehow the ice melted and the salmon leaped up, its body twisting in midair, so I was able to answer her with confidence.

"That's right," I said. "If you don't place the knife at just the right angle, your slices won't be clean. You have to be careful how much strength you use, too."

"And before you go to bed, you wipe all the moisture off the knife and wrap it in *sarashi*, right?"

"*Sarashi*?"

"I wish I'd been born in a country with a traditional culture."

She told me her parents were Danes who had moved to America when they were young. She herself had been born in Texas, and was now traveling through Europe. She probably mistook me for a native of the land of sushi because she'd never seen an Eskimo before. But even if it was based on a misunderstanding, her interest in me, and the way she kept asking me all these questions, felt pretty good. Being singled out as an exotic was a lot more fun than being neutral, just another Eskimo everyone ignored. My Indian friend Anira said the same sort of thing. She'd come to Copenhagen because she was fed up with London. There have always been lots of Indians living in London, so nobody noticed her walking down the street. Which didn't mean they treated her the same as any other woman. The minute people saw her a light would go on in their eyes, like they were thinking, *Oh, another Indian,* that being all they needed to know. After dealing with Indians for four hundred years, English people assumed they had nothing to learn from Anira. Though most of them actually knew nothing about Indian culture, they didn't even think it was worth being curious about. So while she didn't feel they were prejudiced against her, she was invisible in a way, a sort of second-class citizen. In Copenhagen, on the other hand, there aren't many Indians, so people were always asking her about India. And since Denmark has no dark past of ruling India as a colony, Danes have no guilty conscience to put the brakes on their innocent curiosity. "Some people say that asking an Indian too many questions about India is a kind of prejudice," Anira laughed, "but that kind of prejudice I don't mind at all."

I watched the people working at Samurai on the sly. The boy who brought my tea could have been from Greenland. And without his glasses, the guy at the cash register would have looked just like a childhood friend of mine.

The next day I went back to the restaurant and sat at the counter, though there were plenty of empty seats at tables this time. The guy out front pressing rice into little oblongs, then putting slices of raw fish on top, was talking in English to another guy filling bowls with miso soup back in the kitchen. When I asked the guy out front, "Why don't you speak to each other in your native language?" he laughed and said, "I'm American, and he's Vietnamese." "Then could an Eskimo work here?" I asked. "Sure," he said. "We're shorthanded at the moment, so I bet the boss will be happy to hire you." With that, it was settled. Between classes at the language school, I started working part-time at Samurai. And then, soon enough, I was actually fitting a class now and then in between shifts at Samurai.

Since I was naturally good at languages, thanks to the genes I got from my parents, no matter how many classes I skipped my Danish kept getting better until I could not only have a normal conversation, but had also learned how to use difficult words and phrases I'd picked up from newspapers and technical books. I spoke English to the guys I worked with in the restaurant, and I started spicing it up with new accents and vocabulary, so I could pass myself off as a young businessman from Hong Kong, or a budding musician from California.

I didn't tell Mrs. Nielsen about my new part-time job, though. Not that I thought I was doing anything wrong, I just didn't want her to worry. If she knew how interested I was in cooking and restaurant management, she'd start to think I was planning to give up on the university altogether.

At first I worked mainly as a waiter, which was boring, although I had fun talking to customers who believed I was from the land of sushi. When they asked what city I was from, I always told them either Tokyo or Kyoto at first, since those were the only cities I knew, but that got boring, too, so after a little research, I added Shimonoseki and Asahikawa to my list. Once when a customer took a chopstick rest out of her handbag and asked me what it was called I broke into a cold sweat. After that, I got myself a dictionary so I could teach myself the names of common objects like that. I sat in on intensive courses in German and French, and got so I could speak them pretty well, too. But no matter how good I got at European languages, no one would ever believe that I was from Europe. Learning a new language that would give me a second identity at the same time was much more fun. Of course a native speaker would be able to tell as soon as I said *hashioki* that it wasn't my native language, but I was pretty sure I could trick the people around me.

Yes, the idea of getting an extra identity just by learning a new language was exciting. To tell the truth, "identity" is another one of those big words I learned from George. I wasn't ashamed of being an Eskimo, but a whole life with just one identity seemed kind of dull.

Hashioki, urushi, miso-shiru, wakame, kombu, negi. Words that make a strange kind of music. Sounds from far away, yet familiar somehow. Saying them almost brought back scenes from my childhood. Yet just as I was about to see those scenes, as pictures in my head, they disappeared.

As I got used to working at Samurai, they let me go back into the kitchen, where I washed pots and pans, and prepped the ingredients ready for cooking. Cho, the chef from Fujian Province in China, was very talkative, and knew about lots of different things. He was always starting up conversations with me, so I never had to worry about making a nuisance of myself if I asked him a question. He told me how to make the best dashi for miso soup, about all the different kinds of seaweed, about various kinds of fish and how to prepare them, and everything else I asked about. Then at night in bed, I'd write it all down in my notebook. Cho was happy to share what he knew with me.

Once when I asked Cho who had taught him all this stuff, like how to press rice into little oblongs for sushi, or what to boil to make dashi for miso-shiru, or how to make perfect agedashi tofu, he told me he'd learned it all from a French chef at a hotel where he'd worked in Paris. I was shocked. "When the original no longer exists," he said, "there's nothing you can do except look for the best copy," which sounded to me like some sort of riddle—such a scary one that I couldn't bring myself to ask him what it meant.

Lots of customers who came to Samurai asked me about Buddhism. It seemed as if every Danish woman had a miniature Buddha somewhere at home or in her office, and when they came to the restaurant they'd bend their fingers into complicated shapes and ask me, "What does this mudra mean?" Since many of them practiced zazen, too, sometimes a woman would say, "I can't seem to get my legs into a full lotus position. Is it possible to achieve satori with a half lotus?" As the research I did on the internet broadened my knowledge, I was soon able to come up with answers for practically anything they asked me. But something strange kept happening. Whenever I found a good site, it would be gone when I looked for it again a few days later. It seemed to me that as soon as I visited a site, someone noticed and immediately erased it. So I started writing down any important information I found in my notebook right away.

Eskimo genes have a lot in common with people from the land of sushi, so it's natural that our faces should look alike. But for a long time the similarity was hidden beneath the deep snow drifts called history. Eskimo skin was constantly exposed to icy winds, and we ate mainly fish and meat, so we looked different from people from the land of sushi, who ate rice and vegetables and spent more time indoors, studying or working. But as time passed, and we Eskimos switched to living in houses with central heating, eating vegetables and, most importantly, spending more time staring at computer screens, we started looking more and more like them. This is even more true for someone like me, since I'll do anything it takes to make myself look like my favorite anime hero.

My classes at the language school were so easy I was getting bored. When I talked to my teacher, he arranged things so I could take the final exam early. There were still three months until the new term started at the university, so I told Mrs. Nielsen I wanted to travel and widen my horizons, and she not only agreed, but even said she'd pay for my travel expenses. Not by cash, but with digital genomoney. This meant that even in a foreign country I could go to the bank and give them a strand of my hair, which they would use to read my genes, making it possible for me to withdraw money from Mrs. Nielsen's account.

Though I was planning to travel just around Denmark, I soon came to the border with Germany. If it hadn't been for the dogs, I wouldn't have even noticed—I would have just thought it was some old railroad crossing that was no longer used and walked straight over it. But as soon as I crossed a line in the road, three German shepherds came charging out of the bushes, looking pretty fierce. Luckily, the dogs I grew up with were like brothers to me, so I can easily understand their language. Right away they told me they weren't going to attack, so I gave them a big hug and rubbed their heads. "You guys are bored, aren't you?" I said, "You wanna play?" Wagging their tails so hard I was afraid they'd break them off, they licked my cheeks with their long, wet tongues. They used to work for the police, they said, but ever since they'd lost their jobs, they'd been amusing themselves here by playing "guard the border."

I made the rounds of three towns in northern Germany. I'd find a sushi restaurant and ask if I could work there for a while in return for room and board. German pronunciation is clearer than Danish, which made it easier to understand. German sentences were like trains sliding smoothly down the tracks of the grammar already embedded in my mind.

When asked my name, I always answered Tenzo.

I don't know whether Tenzo is actually a name or not, and I never met anyone who knew enough to tell me. I do know that it's the official title of the person in charge of the kitchen in a Zen temple. Vegetarian dishes using seaweed actually interested me more than sushi. Seaweed has a savory taste called umami that leaves you feeling as satisfied as if you'd eaten fish even when you haven't. I'm sure that sometime in the future, when fish are extinct, people will rely on chefs to extract fish traces, distant memories of fish from plants that grow in the sea. That is my project: I call it "Dashi Research." If you read all the way through the long history of Eskimo culture, I'll bet you won't find anyone researching dashi until you get to me.

There's a story I heard at a sushi restaurant in Husum that I can't forget. The place was run by a German guy called Heino Fisch, who was the grandson of the founder, Wolf Fisch. Old Wolf had studied shipbuilding at the University of Kiel as a young man, where he got friendly with some foreign students. One of them was named Susanoo, from a place called Fukui, who told him about sushi, a dish he didn't even know existed until then. The *fuku* of Fukui means *glück* (happiness), a word found in lots of other place names, too, all of which were originally blessed with the riches of nature.

There is a village in Germany called Glückstadt (Happy Town), famous for protests against a nuclear power plant they were going to build about seven miles away. That was a long time ago, but ever since, whenever they hear the name Glückstadt, people think of nuclear power.

Susanoo's home used to be famous for all kinds of seafood—

flat fish, pointed fish, creatures with shells, or with soft bodies and ten legs, or flashy striped dandies, or red revolutionaries, or bottom-feeding creepers with beards—which they scooped up with their nets, some to eat themselves, but most to send to the capital. In time, though, as this coastal area developed in an unhappy direction and became known as Gempatsu Ginza (Nuclear Power Ginza), the fishing industry declined.

Susanoo's family ran a small factory that manufactured robots to take care of old people, but after they took on the job of making all the robots for the display at the Hometown PR Center, money started gushing in like industrial wastewater. Susanoo's father built a big new workshop, and hired new employees. The robots at the Hometown PR Center explained to the children about the different methods of fishing as they threw their nets into a pool, or landed a big tuna with a pole and line. With no more human fishermen around, these robots were the only way to give the kids a clear image of what life had been like in the past. Since there were hardly any farmers left, either, they also made farming robots to push the planters transplanting young rice shoots into the flooded paddy fields, and also to run the harvesting machines. The display at the Hometown PR Center—with all these robots performing the labors that had once made this area lively and prosperous—was popular with tourists as well.

When he was in high school, Susanoo started having doubts about the Hometown PR Center. Around that time, his father made a new kind of robot, a scientist dressed in a white coat, with a very sincere look on its face. "For the development of human civilization," this robot explained, "we had to give up fishing and farming. There was nothing else we could do." Susanoo couldn't understand why a real human scientist didn't come to answer the kids' questions instead. Or for that matter, why not a real politician? Weren't the adults just using a robot, a machine with no sense of right or wrong, having it lie for them so they wouldn't have to take any responsibility? Susanoo hated the idea of making lying robots like his father, so he decided to build big ships that could carry passengers all over the world. That's why he went to the University of Kiel, famous for its course in ship-building, but when he got there he met Wolf, a new friend he went fishing with, or sailing, or on long hiking trips. The more time he spent in nature, the more fed up he got with machines. After graduating, he didn't go home, but stayed on in Husum, where he and Wolf started a restaurant. Looking for something new to try, their curiosity and sense of adventure led them to choose sushi, though at first it was just one item on the menu, along with lots of pork dishes. They started it for fun, really, but the restaurant turned out to be very popular, full of customers every night.

Life went on that way, calm but busy, until suddenly one day Susanoo went off to the south of France. Left alone, Wolf swallowed his grief as he grilled pork and made sushi the way Susanoo had taught him. Eventually he married and had three children; the youngest took over the restaurant until some of Wolf's grandchildren took it over from him. The year before, Wolf had died. Though Susanoo hadn't contacted them in all these years, he might still be alive. "Why did Susanoo suddenly go to the south of France?" I asked. "He was seduced by a woman from Arles and followed her home," Wolf's grandson answered with a shrug of his shoulders. "But anyway, I feel sorry for him now, and for you, too. After all, your country has been wiped out. Do you keep in touch with your countrymen living abroad? Do you have some kind of a network?" I was so surprised I could hardly breathe.

I'd never been to the land of sushi, and didn't know anyone there, so I wasn't all that sad, but, just when I'd chosen it as my second home, finding out it didn't exist anymore was the pits.

Plus everyone must have known that it was gone, and all this time they'd been secretly pitying me.

Maybe it was just a rumor. The land of sushi could be isolated for political reasons, cut off from the rest of the world. I wanted to meet that guy called Susanoo, and hear what he had to say. Arles seemed awfully far away, but I was already heading south. Now I felt like I'd have to keep on going. That was it—I'd go to Arles.

Sometimes the word "south" started multiplying in my brain while I was asleep at night. "South" turned into weeds that kept sprouting up no matter how many times I cut them down, growing taller and thicker until they wrapped themselves around the outside of the room, trapping me inside, unable to open the door while the room kept getting hotter and wetter, the walls were dripping, making me dizzy, smelling the odor of sweat pouring from my pores, and then when the smell changed to semen I heard the squalling of new born babies all around me. And all those kids were mine.

Sometimes in the evening after work I'd go for a walk along the port in Husum, and stand there for hours watching the light from the boats shining like bright pillars on the water. Every town in northern Germany is pretty in its own way, but after a while they all look the same. And I was starting to think northern Germany wasn't all that different from Denmark. I was ready for something completely different.

One night, a customer left a novel on his chair. It was an old paperback with the cover folded back, the yellowed pages soft as cloth. I kept it by the cash register, planning to return it when he came back, but I started leafing through it in my spare time, and was soon hooked. It was a sort of historical romance novel, set at the time of the Roman Empire. One passage in particular caught my eye: "The barbarian girl captured Julius's heart, and their love continued to grow, just like the Roman Empire, which kept on expanding, beyond all boundaries. Yet Roman territory was surrounded by a gray zone, where it was difficult to tell the Emperor's subjects from outsiders. Maintaining its ambiguity, this gray zone also continued to grow. Thus in time, barbarians from the hinterlands entered the center of Rome, where they sometimes succeeded in rising to the most powerful positions." If this kind of society still existed, I wanted to go there. It couldn't have completely disappeared, even if this story happened a long time ago. I was sure I'd find the Roman Empire somewhere in Europe if I looked for it hard enough.

That night a storm was growling through the streets, so despite the Open sign, no one came in. Then the rain started lashing down. When we'd been open about an hour, a customer suddenly rushed in, gasping for breath like someone was chasing him, his black coat shiny with rain. It was the guy who'd forgotten the novel. He took off his coat and hung it on a hook, then sat down way at the back and ordered sake and a California roll. He looked depressed. But when I handed him his book along with a bottle of sake and a little cup to drink it from, he brightened up and started talking as if we were old friends. "Have you been working here long?" he asked. "You know, I don't really care for shrimp, or shellfish, or squid, or salmon roe. What I like best in sushi is avocado, followed by rolled omelet, and salmon's about the only kind of fish I like. I guess that makes me a real dud in your eyes, as a sushi patron anyway, but I still like this place." I didn't have anything else to do, so I decided to keep him company.

Fabian—that was his name—was thirty years old, and came from Trier, though somehow he'd ended up working in northern Germany. I always thought boasting about your hometown was something old folks past fifty did, but this guy Fabian went on about Trier like it was a lover he couldn't get out of his head even though they were far apart. Maybe something bad happened that day to make him suddenly long for home.

He told me about this building in Trier called the Basilica. Just standing in front of it made you feel like you were living in the Roman Empire, he said. In Husum he didn't feel like he was really living. After work he'd go back to his apartment to sleep, and that was all. But just thinking about the Basilica he could feel the paving stones under his feet, and the rough stone of the walls against his hands. Then there'd be sights and smells all around him—of earth mixed with iron; blinding sunlight and deep green leaves; the aroma of meat grilling and of strong wine; pungent vinegar; and the smell of women's bodies. Trier had lots of old ruins like that—just standing in them would take you to another world. As I listened to Fabian, I knew I had to get to Trier.

I left Husum and hitchhiked to Trier. A truck driver who hardly said a word took me as far as Fulda, but after that I couldn't find a ride going straight toward Trier, so I ended up zigzagging my way there. The last car that picked me up was an Audi, but the driver suddenly stopped in the middle of a big, grassy field. "I've got to go see my mother," he said. "She lives at the end of this little road to the left here. I was going to skip this visit, but I've suddenly changed my mind. Sorry, but you'll have to get out here." It was already getting dark, and since it didn't seem like another car would be coming any time soon, I asked if I could tag along, but he coldly refused. He was probably going to see a married woman whose husband was away.

Hoping to find a warm barn where I could spend the night, I walked slowly along the road until I saw the lights of a car coming my way. I jumped out into the middle of the street and waved my arms like windshield wipers. The car stopped, the brakes letting out a metallic scream. The driver was dressed like a businessman, with blond hair, cut short. "Can I please have a ride?" I begged like I was about to start crying. When he asked where I was headed, I told him honestly that I wanted to go to Trier. His face stiffened, then twisted into a smile as he said, "Well, that's a coincidence. Come on, hop in."

Assuming that meant he was on his way to Trier, too—what else could he mean by "coincidence"?—I felt very lucky as I got into the car.

He told me nothing about himself except that his name was Julius, and didn't ask me why I was going to Trier, or where I was from like most people would have. Looking out at the sea of dark grass spread out on either side of the road, I was struck by the blackness of a world without snow. Sometimes little animals would jump into the pool of light in front of the car and then run off, barely managing to escape; I saw myself in their dark shadows. After a while I got drowsy, then fell fast asleep. When I woke up the car had stopped and the driver had disappeared. It was pitch black outside. There were no houses around, and I could barely make out the shadows of the trees. I figured the driver must be off taking a leak somewhere, but no matter how long I waited he didn't come back. What was his name—Julius? With a sense of dread, I opened the glove compartment, which had no maps or papers in it, just ashes, a whole cupful of them. My nose so full of the smell I could hardly breathe, I slammed it shut and got out of the car. A slight smell of smoke was mixed in with the cold night air. I looked through the car window and saw that the rucksack I'd left lying on the back seat was gone. But would he steal something like that and run away, leaving the car? Not a chance. There was nothing in it anyway except some clean clothes and a few books. Then, with a shock, I remembered a mystery I had once read. Maybe Julius had tried to claim all the loot from a robbery for himself and had been escaping when his gang caught up with him, dragged him out of the car... and maybe he was lying somewhere in a field right now, bleeding. Maybe the gang thought my rucksack was full of stolen goods, and took it with them when they escaped. I couldn't think of any other explanation.

Leaving the car door open, I started to walk. I saw a dim light on the horizon. That was the only landmark in sight. The darkness weighing heavily on my shoulders, my knees shaking with worry and fear, my head empty, I made my way down the road in a daze.

Just as the sky was getting light, I saw a sign for Trier. Here and there houses began to appear, I heard car engines, and birds chirping, their voices so shrill they stabbed my brain. A woman riding past on a bicycle stopped ahead of me, and putting a foot down to steady herself, looked back and asked, "Are you all right?" Forcing a smile, I answered, "I stayed too long in a bar last night and I'm really regretting it now. But I live near here, so I'll be fine." I wanted to lie down, but there were no benches, and I didn't see any signs for hotels, either.

Then I saw the old, stone walls of public baths from the Roman Empire, right in front of me. I thought I was in a dream. Before I knew it I was inside. The stone steps had an ancient sheen to them. At the bottom of those stairs were the baths, where men wrapped in white cloth would be drinking wine as they talked about politics. I heard the regular drip, drip, drip of water on stone. That's when my vision blurred, the strength drained from my legs, and I fell, rolling down the stairs and twisting my ankle. There weren't so many steps, but when I got to the bottom of them and tried to stand up, I felt a stabbing pain in my ankle and howled like a dog. Furthermore, someone had started stirring my brains with a spoon. Dragging my aching foot, I tried to limp further back toward the baths, but my strength gave out and I fainted.

I found out later that I had been in a place called the Kaiserthermen, the actual ruins of the old Roman baths. Nora, who came and helped me, wasn't like any woman I had ever met before. She had the power to make everything around her bend to her will. When Nora held a blanket in her hands it became her servant and set to work, warming me up. A bandage didn't look like one until Nora called it by its name: "bandage." When she came into a room, suddenly I was in a space that her body filled, while the furniture and windows faded into the background like illustrations in a book. I was overwhelmed. All the adjectives I had casually used to describe girls until then, like "cute" or "sweet" or "pretty," now became so light that a breeze blew them out of my mind.

Without really thinking I'd put my hand on the table, and when Nora placed hers on top of it, the table, now pregnant, would start shining from inside as the Mosel River flowed from an overturned glass, and points of light—children, too many to count—would dance across the water. They were our family.

I was soaking in a river of delight, yet at the same time I was afraid of turning into a piece of Nora's miniature Roman Empire, under her control I couldn't tell anymore whether I did things because I wanted to, or because Nora had planned it that way. The only place I could really be myself was in memories of my old life, before I came to Copenhagen. Fixed in her belief that I was from the land of sushi, Nora never noticed that I was an Eskimo.

It's really scary when two people blend into one. While I watched Nora sip her coffee, I tasted it in my own mouth. I woke up when she did. When Nora was hungry, my stomach started growling. The two of us were one. That's why it was enough for Nora to have a proper job, while I couldn't find one. This had never happened to me before. I was getting desperate. I couldn't even buy a banana without getting money from Nora. I could have taken money from Mrs. Nielsen's account, but the day when I'd promised to be back in Copenhagen was long past, and if things went on this way I'd be guilty of scholarship fraud. Was it Nora who was holding me hostage, or the Roman Empire? I had to free myself and get back to northern Europe as soon as possible.

Realizing how depressed I was at not being able to find a job, Nora told me about the Umami Festival. I was sure I'd be able to give an interesting talk on umami, and since I didn't want to keep on staying with Nora like some kind of parasite I said I'd take part. One thing worried me, though. If someone who really was from the land of sushi showed up at the festival, what would I do? I'd be exposed. And when Nora found out what a liar I was, she'd ditch me. Strangely enough, the more I felt I had to get away from her, the more afraid I was that she'd leave me and finally I couldn't stand it anymore.

Feeling trapped, I spent many sleepless nights thinking about how to make my escape until finally I told Nora I had to go to Oslo. That way, even if the break wasn't final, I could put some distance between us for the time being. I scoured the internet, and discovered this place in Oslo, a real restaurant called Shinise Fuji, where they were having a competition for chefs. If I flew to Copenhagen and Nora came after me she'd find out who I really was, and to get to Arles I'd have to first take the train to Paris, which was also dangerous because she'd be sure to come and see me off at the station, and might even force her way onto the train. I didn't want to go as far as Mumbai or Hong Kong, and didn't have enough money anyway. Norway was just the right distance away.

Much later I realized that my real reason for choosing Norway had nothing to do with all these different factors. The first two letters of *Norway* are *No*, which expressed my feelings exactly.

As I looked up at the sky, blue came deep inside me and emptied me out. The square windows on a snow-white five-story building stared down at me like a robot's eyes, that same blue reflected in the glass; perhaps there were people living behind those windows but I didn't know them and probably never would. The building next door was deep red, about the same height but much more rhythmical, with glassed-in balconies at regular intervals along the outside. Each veranda had a little table where people could sit quietly sipping tea, pretending not to hear the cars below, but in this city, full of logical angles and lines that suppressed all signs of violent emotion while at the same time deftly avoiding ugliness, I didn't know anyone well enough to sit on a veranda with them.

Passersby walked casually down the street, a little too fast. The shops were dark inside, or had their shutters down. Sharp-eyed men looked out from parked cars.

Something seemed odd from the time I arrived at Oslo Airport. Policemen were standing around in the terminal building, and there was a long line in front of a counter marked "Border." Normally there is no immigration inspection for travelers within Scandinavia.

"Your passport has expired."

"renewal impossible."

"Why?"

"country vanished. residence permit for denmark have."

I handed all the documents I had with me to the inspector. When I'm talking to government officials, my Panska sounds very fragile. I made this language by gathering threads just strong enough to get my meaning across, but now I was afraid its beauty would be trampled by the sheer force of authority.

"Your job?"

"märchen center."

"Do you work in the office?"

"animals on paper draw. to immigrant children stories tell."

He must have gotten fed up listening to my explanation, because he turned away and loudly stamped my passport.

Men in uniforms, carrying guns, were stationed along the corridor. Judging from their uniforms, they were not policemen, but soldiers. I kept my head down so I wouldn't have to look at them. My legs felt stiff, as if encased in invisible plaster casts.

When I got off the train in front of a theater, I saw a kiosk outside the station. Behind the colorful packets of gum and newspaper photos was a fresh-faced young girl with clusters of freckles like constellations, making her even prettier. When I asked her how to get to the restaurant "Shinise Fuji," she looked it up on a map and marked it for me.

"thank you," I said. "norwegians very kind."

"There are killers here too," her face twisting into a frown: "Take care!" That was not something I was expecting to hear.

In a corner of this city, a constant struggle between land and water, I found a large terrace made of reddish brown wood. An octagonal building with glass walls was perched on top of it like a young girl with her skirt spread out around her. The roof looked like a *kaku obi*, the stiff sash men wear with kimono. I had almost forgotten that word, *kaku obi*. Perhaps meeting Tenzo would stir up the pond in my brain, bringing more words that had sunk to the bottom floating back up to the surface.

Drawing near I saw a sign that said Restaurant, though it didn't seem to be open. Through the glass I watched young men and women dressed in black construct a low stage in one corner. Toward the back was a counter, and behind it was a noren, a split curtain with the word "sushi" on it. *Noren* was another word I hadn't used for a long time. In the kitchen behind the noren a man wearing a bandana was working alone. I pressed my nose against the glass, wondering if he might be Tenzo, but he soon disappeared.

I saw a policeman walking toward me reflected in the glass. Even though I had nothing to feel guilty about, I hurried into the restaurant as if he were chasing me.

A boy moving tables glanced over at me. "ten-zo here?" I asked him, pronouncing the name "Tenzo" slowly and clearly. Expressionless, the young man shook his head. "event here to-night? what kind?" He just shrugged his shoulders, so I gave up and went outside.

There were no more men in uniform, which was a relief, so I sat down on a bench and, picking up a newspaper someone had left behind, started to read. The photo on the front page was of people in orange work clothes hunched over gray ruins, cleaning up wreckage. There had been an explosion. I put the newspaper down and sought refuge in the restaurant. Two young men were lining up chairs. I waited there a long time, but Tenzo did not appear, nor did Knut or Nora. As it was getting dark outside, I decided to look for a place to stay.

When I asked a young man taking a coffee break at the counter if he knew of a cheap hotel, he whipped out a pencil and quickly drew me a map. It had been a long time since I had met someone who could dash off a map that way. Perhaps he was an architecture student. The lines were all perfectly straight, and the street names easy to read. If I followed this map, I couldn't possibly get lost. The houses that lined both sides of the street looked more like well-dressed teenagers than nouveaux riches. Money to spare, but spent with modesty and good taste.

But after a while I came to a house that stood out like a child from the only poor family in the neighborhood. It was a low, single-story building, made not of brick or concrete, but wood. The siding, once deep red, was badly faded, and the white paint on the window frames was peeling off, with painful looking splinters in the wood. When buildings now seem to be competing to see who can use the most glass, the windows in this one looked very small and cloudy. I peered inside and saw a room with a low ceiling and a man with a beard sitting near the back. Around to the side I found the entrance, with the five letters HOTEL in chalk, written in a child's uneven scrawl.

I screwed up my courage to ring the bell but as there wasn't one, I knocked. A reply came from inside, and though I couldn't even tell what language it was, since people don't usually say "Keep out" to a knock on the door, I figured it must mean "Come in," and pushed the door open. Once inside, I suddenly remembered that some people will growl "Nobody's here" when someone knocks, but it was too late to back out now.

The man's skin was smooth and ruddy; his beard hanging down from his chin like icicles. He was staring intently at a sketchbook that lay open on the oak table. When I walked over, he didn't look up. Perhaps I shouldn't have come in after all. In this city where I knew no one, I somehow had to find a place to stay before nightfall, and my anxiety made me bold.

"hostel?" I asked, and the man nodded and, pointing to a door at the back with his chin, said, "Room 3." A man of few words.

When I opened that door at the back, the ceiling seemed even lower. Small doors were lined up on both sides. Looking closely, I saw that each door had a marker about the size of a postage stamp with the room number on it, but the numbers were irregular—1, 9, 2, 6—so it took me a while to find Number 3.

It was the door at the very end, with a key sticking out of its keyhole. Though the window was too small to let in much light from the outside, perhaps because of the warm glow coming from the wood, the room didn't feel dark.

Leaving my bag on the chair in the room, I went back to where the man was to find the sketchbook closed, and a picture postcard lying on the cover. When I bent over for a closer look my eyes met the man's; embarrassed, I quickly looked away, but he handed me the postcard.

It was a winter scene. The snow was tinged with yellow, a sweet color. There was a magpie, perched on what looked like a broken ladder. My eyes stopped on the soft feathers that hid the bird's legs and stayed there, staring.

"What are you looking at?"

I raised my head to find that the man was looking at me, his eyes filled with curiosity. I suddenly began to speak, a flood of Panska.

"this bird legs does not have. artist did not draw. I, too, legs left out when crane I drew. colleague said, 'duck.' legs I added. 'crane,' colleague said. but making colleague see crane is not art. i was wrong."

The man looked at me in surprise and, as if he had just noticed that someone was standing there, stuck out his right hand and said, "Claude." Shaking his hand, I said, "hiruko." His Norwegian was easy to understand.

"My ancestors came to Oslo from the south of France," he said. "The light here is very beautiful. So is Mediterranean light, but it's too comfortable, placid, lazy, muddy. Scandinavian light is transparent, always changing, second by second."

"why oslo?"

"Because Mt. Fuji is here."

This gave me a jolt. Mt. Fuji couldn't be in Oslo. But then again, there could be more than one Mt. Fuji. After all, Nora had called the restaurant Nise Fuji—fake Fuji—by mistake. I could accept the real one being one place and a copy somewhere else. But what if the one here was the only one? Too frightened to ask why Mt. Fuji was in Oslo, I simply said, "going out. meet friends," and left.

I wasn't lying when I said I was going to meet friends. Thinking I might see Knut, I practically ran. A police officer and a man in a suit were standing in front of the restaurant, talking. Their brows were furrowed, their faces like gloved hands picking up explosives. The policeman finally nodded and walked away, while the other man turned on his heel and went into the restaurant. I stood there, wondering whether or not to go in. Then someone slapped me on the shoulder from behind, startling me, and when I turned around, I saw Nora standing there.

Nora's a whole head taller than me, and sturdily built. The rhythm of the English she spouted out suggested considerable lung capacity, too—this was someone I could depend on. I'm not *hitoribocchi* (alone), I have friends, I thought. Then I suddenly wasn't sure if *bocchi* was really a word.

"Hello, Hiruko! When did you arrive? Have you been waiting long? Where are the others?"

"Knut isn't here yet."

"How about Tenzo?"

"He's probably not here either. But I never met him so I don't know what he looks like."

"Let's go inside. It'll get cold when the sun sets."

In the restaurant, Nora sat down on the first chair she came to. I sat down next to her, but she was in such a state, talking on and on, that I slid my chair back to put some distance between us.

"I was really shocked when Tenzo left," Nora said. "I wasn't expecting it at all. But looking back, I think I might have seen it coming. The distance between us shrank so very quickly. Too quickly, perhaps. So I can imagine him feeling a desire to escape."

Unable to ride the waves of her words, I found my mind wandering on to other topics. I thought about the terrorist incident in this city, about the man at the hostel and Mt. Fuji, and about myself, waiting anxiously for Knut. It would have been perfectly natural for me to be thinking mainly about Tenzo. When he came, I would be able to speak my native language for the first time in years. After all, that was the purpose of this trip. My past was now much too far away to reach out and touch. But soon, someone would be standing in front of me who understood my native language, the one I used to breathe in along with the air that filled my lungs, that would go down my gullet along with the sweet-and-sour taste of soy sauce and mirin and seep into the cotton lining of my stomach, and then slip into my veins to be carried in a constant stream up to my brain.

When I talked to Tenzo, even for a few minutes, all the countless threads that connected us would show themselves. Those threads were words.

It was the ebb and flow of hormones that connected Nora to Tenzo, so what would their meeting be like? The way she talked about him, as if she were moaning in ecstasy, got on my nerves so I moved my chair even further back. That was when I saw a sliver of water between the brown of the terrace boards and the bright blue of the sky.

The color of the water changed from moment to moment, from a deep blue to a lighter shade tinged with green, and then to a blue that was almost gray. The clouds were always moving, changing the color of the water reflecting them. Could the expression on a person's face make such delicate changes?

Nora noticed that I wasn't listening to her. "What are you thinking about?" she asked. "Are you worried about something?" Her voice, awfully sticky before, now sounded much cleaner.

"People's feelings always changing; sad one minute then happy. Like sky here. Sky changes, color of water reflects changes, too."

I realized that though I was speaking English, my sentences were getting closer to Panska, but I had no intention of fixing this. I've never spoken English very well, and didn't want to give the impression that I was fluent. Panska, on the other hand, was my own homemade language, a work of art I'd poured my whole self into, Panska was me, and I couldn't give in to other people every time my brush hit the canvas. Seen up close, my brush-strokes might look like rough, meaningless blobs. But if you stepped back to look at the whole canvas, you'd see a beautiful pond with water lilies.

"You know water lilies of Monet," I said. "People's emotions appear in pond more than faces. But water is not enough. Light also needed."

I stepped into the gallery in my mind and examined each of the paintings hanging there. When the sky is a vivid blue, green gleams all the more brightly. These two colors should blend nicely since they're next to each other, yet there's a hidden friction between them, so they almost seem to be fighting. Though the sky reflected in the pond and the water lilies floating on it look as if they're touching on the canvas, in reality they never do. There's something mysterious about the way all this can be expressed in a painting that only exists on a thin canvas surface.

Nora couldn't get Tenzo out of her head, so she associated water lilies more with Buddhism than with Monet. "The Buddha sits on a water lily, does he not?" she suddenly asked, startling me. "Why is that?"

"Water lily blooms in marsh," I answered, remembering an explanation I happened to overhear long ago. "World under Buddha's feet is secular swamp." Very impressed, Nora nodded again and again, but in my mind's eye Monet's lily pond was clear, not at all like a swamp. I told Nora I had to go to the restroom.

A mirror is not a pond. While I was washing my hands, I looked into the mirror and saw another pond, one that made the years fall away as I stared into its depths, so that when I came to myself I had gone far into the future, and no one I knew was around anymore. Wasn't there a fairy tale like that? About a boy who saves a turtle from a gang of kids throwing stones at it. I couldn't remember his name. Was it Kametarō? Or Prince Ryūgū? After enjoying himself for some time in Ryūgū, the Dragon Palace, the boy comes back to his village to find every-thing changed. And sometimes when you come back from the toilet, you discover that the people you left behind have changed in ways you can't explain.

This was true of Nora—everything had changed for her. There was now a young man standing across from her. Nora was speaking softly, her head tilted to one side, but every time she reached out to take his arm, the man quickly turned to one side and took a step backward. Though they were almost the same height, Nora looked taller. As they were speaking German, the only word I understood was "umami." Feeling guilty about standing there listening, I cleared my throat before going nearer, and when she noticed me, Nora's face lit up.

"May I introduce you? This is Tenzo," she said encouragingly in English, looking from Tenzo to me and back again. "And this is Hiruko. You are both from the same country." The phrase "from the same country" spun around in empty circles. Wary as a wildcat, the young man looked searchingly at me. "Tenzo, finally here's someone you can talk to in your native language. Pretend I'm not here, and go ahead, talk to Hiruko." Nora was the only cheerful one, egging us on.

"*Ha-ji-me-MA-shite*," he said with an awkward smile. His pro-nunciation was stilted. An explosive *ha* hit the air, followed by *ji*, which sounded more like *ju*, he put too much emphasis on *ma*, then rolled down the hill on *shite*. I fondly remembered that old-fashioned word "foreigner." It had probably fallen out of use by now. Was Tenzo some kind of foreigner? Not necessarily.

Remembering a boy I knew back in junior high school who got so nervous when he talked to girls that he sounded like a foreigner, I said, "So you're Tenzo. I've heard that you and some other chefs are going to be comparing skills here in this restaurant." But "comparing skills" sounded awfully old-fashioned, like that folktale about the fox and the tanuki who compare their shape-shifting skills. What would you call an event with a bunch of chefs all trying to beat the others by cooking the best meal? A surprising number of people would wiggle their way out by borrowing the English word "competition." Though that seemed awfully lazy to me, I went ahead and used it anyway. "There's going to be a dashi competition?" I asked.

Tenzo's face relaxed. "Yes there is," he said. "*Gam-bari-masu.* (I'll do my best)." Years ago I'd heard that *gambaru* had fallen out of use, but Tenzo must have been living abroad for a long time.

He spoke with a strong accent, unlike any I had heard before. It didn't sound anything like the Hokuetsu dialect my grandparents used to speak. Tomi-chan, my best friend from elementary school, was from Osaka, but Tenzo's rhythm was completely different from hers, too. Wondering where he was from, I asked, "Where is your *o-kuni*?"

"*O-kuni*? My country? Don't have one."

So that was it—our country had vanished, and he had never lived in any prefecture long enough to call it home. I used to envy people like that when I was a child. Kids who changed schools a lot because their parents were bankers, or beekeepers, or judges, or traveling actors, so rhythms and accents from all over were mixed together into a special blend echoing in their speech.

Putting her hand on Tenzo's shoulder, Nora said something to him in German. I couldn't understand her, but she seemed to be saying something like, "What's wrong? Don't be so shy. Go ahead and talk."

Tenzo looked at me gravely, like a student eyeing the proctor giving him an exam. That made it hard for me to talk naturally. If he and I were old friends, I could just go back to the way we used to talk. But I was meeting him for the first time, and I couldn't imagine what sort of conversation would be natural in a case like this. What's more, I could feel how tense Tenzo was, looking straight at me, determined not to miss a single word I said, making it all the harder to talk naturally.

"The competition—when is it?" I was now speaking as if I were talking to someone who had just started to learn the language, pronouncing each word slowly and clearly, without adding any extra flourishes.

"Tomorrow more-ning ten o'clock is when."

Somewhere, sometime I had heard that sort of grammatical construction. The answer to "Who?" would be "Suzuki-san is who," or to "Where?" "Tokyo is where." I couldn't remember exactly when I'd heard it now, but it definitely wasn't a dialect—I think it was the influence of some foreign language. Also, Tenzo seemed to have trouble saying the word "morning," drawing the first syllable out so that it sounded more like "more-ning." I remembered hearing a Scandinavian student pronounce it the same way. So to Tenzo, "morning" was a foreign word. He hadn't been speaking my native language as a child. Yet for some reason, he didn't want Nora to know that.

"Do you have a *yado*?" I asked, then realizing he might not know the word "yado," rephrased my question. "Do you have a hotel?" Nora recognized the word "hotel."

"That's right," she said. "We have to look for a hotel. I don't have a place to stay yet, either." She looked down at her suitcase. I told her in English about the hostel I'd found, and about the strange old man with French ancestors.

"That sounds like an interesting place. I'd like to stay there, too, but where will you stay, Tenzo?"

Tenzo pointed his chin toward the back of the restaurant. The two of them talked in German. I imagined that Nora was saying she wanted to stay at the restaurant, too, and Tenzo was telling her that that wouldn't be possible. Looking out of sorts, Nora turned to me and said, "I'll go to that hostel you mentioned and check in now, so tell me where it is." When I took the map that young man had drawn for me out of my pocket, it was crinkled up like a crying face. Shoulders back, chest thrown out, Nora strode off, her suitcase following her like a pet dog.

Left alone, Tenzo and I looked at each other.

"You've been playacting for Nora, haven't you?" I said.

"Playing?"

"Plays—Ibsen, Strindberg, Shakespeare ..."

"Oh, play. Nora misunderstands. I do not lie."

"So you mean she took you for someone else, and you never told her she had made a mistake. But why? As a Dashi Meister, is it better to keep her in the dark?"

"Bed her to keep? No."

"You're a cook, aren't you?"

"At sushi bar in Germany worked. But dashi more interesting than sushi."

"Why are you tricking Nora this way? You keep playacting—why?"

"Second identity very convenient. Very happy."

When I speak Panska, it must sound to the Scandinavians the way Tenzo sounds to me right now, I thought.

"Is Tenzo your real name?" I asked.

"No."

"Then tell me. What is your real name?"

"I am called Nanook. A poor and humble man am I, but please treat me well in the future."

"The textbook you're using must be awfully old," I said. "But Nanook is a nice name. Are you from Greenland?"

"The scenery in Greenland is very beautiful. Please come to visit sometime."

"You got that sentence straight out of your textbook. Did you study by yourself? I would really like to visit Greenland someday, though. When I was a child, I had a book about an Eskimo boy. I read it over and over again, until it fell apart. The boy in the story could talk to sea otters. And he looked just like the boy who lived next door to me. It's funny, you know. When I think about my childhood, the people I read about in my picture books seem just as real as the people I actually knew. I had books about people from lots of different places. And animals, too—lots of them. So maybe the land of picture books is my real home."

Nanook looked at me in a daze. The stream of words washing over him seemed to feel good, whether or not he understood them. "I'm really glad I met you, though," I went on. "It doesn't matter if you don't understand everything I say. I feel as if these words I'm saying aren't just a meaningless flood of sounds, but a real language. And that's because you're here. Do you mind if I tell Nora who you really are?"

When he heard Nora's name, Nanook looked down, thinking it over a while. "Lie is no good," he said, finally looking up. "I tell Nora truth," he added with a weak smile.

"Yes, it's best you tell her yourself. If I were to tell her, it would be like I was talking behind your back. But cheer up. I don't think lies are necessarily all bad. Plays are lies. But they're art, too. This character Tenzo you created is a work of art. In that sense, Tenzo is the real thing."

Nanook's face brightened up, just a bit. Even if he couldn't understand every word, he was letting his feelings flow along with my words, and seemed to be picking up nuggets of meaning along the way. I was glad I hadn't spoken to him in English.

Just then, what looked like a moth made of red silk came fluttering into the restaurant. It was Akash in his red sari.

"Akash," I said. "What are you doing here? I thought you said you couldn't come to Oslo."

Out of breath, Akash spoke in phrases, splicing them in between gasps: "Heard from Knut ... can't come ... asked me to come in his place ... paid for my ticket."

As soon as I heard Knut wouldn't be coming my lungs grew heavier. Though spring hadn't come to my heart yet, bright yellow and white crocuses had broken through the hard winter earth. You couldn't call it love yet, but I wouldn't be going back to winter. Akash and Nanook stood eyeing each other in wonder.

"Akash," I said, "this is the Dashi Meister Tenzo. His real name is Nanook, though, and he's from Greenland. He's a sushi chef, and worked in sushi bars in Germany, but what he's really interested in is dashi—he's doing research on it."

Akash glowered at Nanook, and suddenly started speaking German. Nanook replied, lowering his voice, trying to sound serious. When he heard what Nanook had said, Akash, his eyebrows slanting downwards like an Ashura, stepped toward him, shooting question after question at him, but Nanook just shrugged his shoulders with a half-hearted laugh. Akash turned bright red, and a slender brown arm suddenly shot out of the red silk to grab Nanook by the collar. I wormed my way in between them.

"What's wrong?" I asked. "What are you talking about? Please translate for me."

As soon as they heard the word "translate" the fire went out of their fight. Nothing makes a fight seem sillier than having to translate something in the middle of it. Akash explained himself in English.

"We have come all this way because of his lies. I told him he should take responsibility for that."

"I lied to Nora," Nanook countered. "But I haven't lied to you."

"Settle down," I sighed, "Let's review our reasons for coming to Oslo. I wanted to meet someone who speaks my native language. Knut said he'd come too because he's a linguist, generally interested in language. Nora came to meet her boyfriend. But Akash, why did you come?"

Looking embarrassed, Akash answered in a whisper. "I want to be Knut's friend."

"But Knut isn't coming. So why are you here?"

"Knut asked me to, and I couldn't say no."

"So you wanted to do what Knut asked, and you did. Why so angry then? And why can't Knut come?"

"His mother is sick. An adopted son or someone left home and hasn't been heard from since, and she's so worried about him that she's become ill. She called Knut and told him to come right away. He refused, telling her he was going to Oslo. But then even though she was supposed to be sick she announced that she was going too, and bought herself a ticket for Oslo. When he heard that, Knut decided not to come. He's very upset about it. But what about Nora, is she here?"

"She went to the hotel to check in. What about you, Akash, do you have a place to stay?"

"I'll be staying with a friend of a friend of a friend. He's from Pune, too."

"That's amazing. You have a network, all around the world — and I can't even find one person from my homeland."

The thought of Nora coming back soon was rather depressing. Akash and I had found out that Tenzo was really Nanook before she did. When she heard that, would she explode in anger and go back to Trier? This strange traveling band of ours might break up if it lost its purpose.

"Tell me again why you're all traveling together," Nanook asked in English.

"Well, people say the country I come from has vanished. I haven't spoken my native language for a long time, so I'm looking for someone from my homeland here in Europe. That's my only reason, really."

"I know someone like that," Nanook shouted, his eyes opening wide, excited, perhaps, at this sudden chance to be helpful. "I heard about him at the sushi bar where I used to work in Husum. He should still be living in Arles."

"What is his name?"

He stared up at the ceiling, trying to remember. "Susanoo, or something like that," he said, not sounding very confident.

"He wasn't from Greenland, was he?"

"No, some town called Fukui."

"Fukui isn't a town, it's more a prefecture. But Susanoo doesn't sound any more like a real person's name than Tenzo."

"I guess it's a really old name. If he's still alive, he must be a very old man."

"Judging from the name, he might even be 2600 years old."

"Huh?"

"I'm joking. Do you have his address?"

"I can ask Heino Fisch, the guy who runs the sushi bar in Husum."

Nora, back from checking in at the hotel, walked toward us with a big smile on her face.

"Hello, Akash," she said. "You'd said you wouldn't be able to come to Oslo, but here you are. I'm so glad. Now the only one missing is Knut."

"Knut isn't coming."

"Why?"

"His mother's sick."

"But Nora," I said, taking her arm, "Tenzo has something important to tell you. Akash and I will leave you two alone. We'll be waiting outside." Nora looked at me as if I'd just handed her a riddle, but rather than explaining anything further, I took Akash by the arm and led him outside.

"I wonder what's going to happen with those two," I said.

"Well," said Akash with a mischievous gleam in his eye, "if you sincerely loved someone, believing him to be Norwegian, then found out one day that he'd been lying to you, and was actually Danish, would you be able to not go on loving him?" That made me feel a little relieved.

"It makes me sad that Knut's not coming."

"Yes. I wish Knut could come, too."

"I wish Knut were here."

"Me too. If only Knut were here ..."

It was comforting, just tossing Knut's name back and forth.

About twenty minutes later, Nanook and Nora came out of the restaurant. Saying nothing about their conversation, Nanook calmly announced, "Many chefs will gather here from ten tomorrow morning until five in the evening for a contest, so please come if you're free." Akash looked as if he had something more to say to him, but Nora was pulling on my arm, dragging me away.

"All right, then," said Akash, finally giving up, "let's meet here at ten o'clock tomorrow morning."

"There's nothing more for us to do here," Nora told us, as if her mind were made up, "so let's go back to the hostel." Stumbling along after her, I somehow managed to keep up. The sun was going down, and I saw a man in a uniform on the corner with a gun. I didn't want to talk about Nanook, so I asked her about terrorism.

"Did you hear anything about a terrorist incident?"

"Terror? Oh, that's right—some racist killed a bunch of people."

"Do you think it's dangerous for someone who looks exotic, like me, to be out on the streets?"

"Probably not. The racist himself was white, and the people he killed were all white, too. He blew up a government building, and then killed a whole lot of young people—Norwegians just like him. I heard about it from someone with a newspaper on my way to the hostel."

"I wonder what will happen tomorrow."

"Who knows?"

"Of course you'll be going tomorrow, won't you? To see Nanook win the competition."

Nora looked troubled but said nothing. When I could no longer bear her silence, I told her what Akash had said about loving someone you thought was Norwegian and then finding out he was really Danish, and was surprised at how quickly she laughed. "I think I can go on loving him," she said, "but it still hurts, being lied to. Besides, now my head is full of Greenland, a place I'd never even thought of before. The world map in my head is shifting around, and it's giving me a headache."

"I'm really looking forward to tomorrow," I said, feeling relieved. "As long as the dashi tastes good, who cares where the person who made it comes from."

When we got back to the hostel, Claude must have gone to bed, because he wasn't around. We decided to follow suit, and went to our rooms.

Beans were roasting in my dream. A good smell. Like a butterfly my nose followed the aroma, breathing it in, letting it seep in from my nose on up to my brain. The smell of coffee. Claude and Nora were already sitting across from each other at the table having breakfast.

"Good morning," I said. "I haven't smelled coffee this good in a long time."

"Smells fade quickly," said Claude. "So does light. In fact, light fades even faster. It grows fainter with every moment. That's why my ancestor used to line up several canvases so that he could capture how the same scene changed along with the shifting of the light. The scene at one o'clock, at one thirty, at two o'clock. He didn't finish one painting and then go on to the next, but kept coming back to the same scene at the same time every day."

But you couldn't be sure you'd be the same painter at one o'clock today that you were at the same time yesterday, I thought, though I didn't say it out loud.

Nora, who had been wearing a fluffy white sweater the day before, now had on a dark green silk blouse with a stand-up collar, and her face was perfectly made up. I never felt like dressing up that way; I'd wear an old gunnysack over my head if I could. I wanted to stroll around town, wrapped in loose, warm cloth. After finally finding peace in Denmark, thinking I could stay there, now here I was traveling again. And like a snowball getting bigger and bigger as it rolls down a hill, I kept picking up more people along the way. If Knut were here, all this meaningless wandering would have a focus again, which would be a relief, but unfortunately he was the one who was missing. I stopped thinking about what would happen next. The days when you could design your future were over. Whether Nanook won or not, today would be a good day: with Nora and Akash, I'd watch him show off his skills as a chef, and afterwards, we'd have a nice dinner together. When I tried to imagine the future that was as far as I got.

But this little prediction of mine, which I was absolutely sure would come true, didn't—not at all. As soon as Nora and I reached the Shinise Fuji, Nanook and Akash came out as if they'd been waiting for us. Their heads down, they headed for the water without so much as a good morning. Since Akash was easier to talk to, I ran after him to find out what was going on.

"What's wrong? The competition's about to start, isn't it?" What I liked about Akash was that even when he was disappointed or angry, he was like a room with the light on, inviting you in.

"The event's been canceled," he said.

"Why?"

"It's complicated. I can't really talk about it here, so let's go to a coffee shop."

I turned around to see Nora talking earnestly to Nanook, while he walked along in silence, his head hanging so far down it looked like his neck would break.

When we reached a nearby coffee shop, Nanook was still too devastated to speak, so Akash explained the situation to us in his bright voice.

The event was sponsored by a hot-tempered man called Breivik, who had an unusually twisted personality for a Norwegian. He'd gotten a phone call from an international environmentalist organization protesting the use of yellowfin tuna in his event because, like the Pacific bluefin tuna, it was endangered. He was enraged. Tuna was tuna, he snorted, and his chefs would use all sorts. Furthermore, he would use this competition to show the world that eating whale meat was an important part of Norway's traditional culture. It was difficult even for ultranationalists like Breivik to explain the difference between Norway's traditional values and those of other European countries. In fact, Norway's long relationship with whales was about its only distinguishing feature.

Perhaps Breivik intended to anger the environmentalists by putting whale meat on display as part of Norway's traditional cooking culture. But having decided on this plan, he had trouble finding chefs who knew how to cook whale meat. Then he heard about this fellow called Tenzo, the only contestant who'd said he knew how prepare several dishes using whale, so, just the day before, he'd decided to start the event off with Tenzo's presentation. That night an advertisement with the provocative slogan "The Joy of Cooking Whale" had been sent out on electronic waves throughout the city.

This morning Breivik had gotten a telephone call from the police ordering him to report for questioning in connection with a dead whale that had washed up on the shore. "You are responsible for this event featuring whale meat cooking, are you not?" they asked when Breivik insisted the competition had nothing to do with the whale's death. "The whale meat I'm using was purchased months ago," he retorted, "and has been stored in the freezer all this time. I can show you the bill of sale." "Besides, what sort of person would plan an event he could only pull off by killing a whale the night before?" Yet though he talked like a bully, Breivik was secretly so terrified of the police that he ended up canceling not only the whale meat presentation but the entire event. And since he couldn't very well ignore the order to report for questioning, he was now on his way to the police station. Around noon, Nanook was also to go in to answer some questions.

"We will go with you." I was once again speaking my native language, using sentences straight out of a language textbook. Nanook must have understood me, because the tension in his face relaxed a bit. "We should all go to the police station with Nanook," I said in English to Nora and Akash. "We may be sure he had nothing to do with the whale's death, but immigrants always have to worry about being arrested for some silly reason or other. So it's best for him to have friends around him."

"Of course I'll go with you," Akash said, smiling like a young girl. Nora nodded—naturally she would join us. Nanook, who had been drooping like a wilted plant, straightened up. Sitting there discussing our plans in English, we were like the four legs of a table that could never wobble or fall over.

But when silence returned, I figured our minds were probably all occupied with entirely different things. Nora surely still had things she wanted to say, not to Nanook, but to Tenzo. They would all concern their sex-drenched relationship, though, so she definitely wouldn't say them here. Akash might be wanting to talk to me about Knut. But as we had actually spent so little time with him, we would both be dreaming of the unknown, merely naming the object of our desire. I also felt I'd like to be alone with Nanook, so we could continue our awkward conversation. I'd been expecting to meet Tenzo, but talking to Nanook might be even better.

As these thoughts were going through my head, I was spreading goat cheese the rich brown of caramel onto Swedish crisp bread, as thick and hard as rice crackers. Nora and Akash had ordered salad, while Nanook just kept asking for more water.

"What's that you're eating?" asked Akash.

"Gjetost," I replied, and when I saw their puzzled looks I realized for the first time that I was the only one here who had actually lived in Norway, if only for a short time. And I wanted to tell that ultranationalist Breivik that of the four people here, I was the closest to being Norwegian.

Nanook spread his notice from the police out on the table and anxiously checked the map. "Tell me what's worrying you," Nora said in English, "If there's anything I can do, tell me and I'll do it. I'll do anything, just ask me …" But all this encouragement seemed to be weighing Nanook down.

When we got to the police station, there were about fifteen young people gathered out front carrying flags and signs. The signs had crude drawings of whales on them. They were even worse than the ones I did for my picture dramas at the Märchen Center. They would have been better off just doing simple illustrations with clean lines, but maybe being Norwegian they all wanted to draw like Munch, and had tried too hard for that distorted, wavy look. Plus they were so afraid their message wouldn't get across that they ended up reducing their whales to a metaphor. They'd drawn them with eyes and mouths open wide in surprise because they were being hit by what looked like radio waves. The waves were coming out of piles of cash.

All of them, both men and women, had long blonde hair, and looked very young, standing there raising and lowering their signs to the rhythm of the slogans they were chanting. When one of them stooped down to tie his shoe, I went over and asked him what the fuss was about.

The whale carcass that had washed up on the beach had no external injuries, he told me. While the police insisted that was evidence of death due to natural causes, it had actually been killed by laser beams used to search for oil deposits deep beneath the sea. Although this method had been banned, since the price of oil had plummeted on the international market, the government was turning a blind eye to the oil companies' illegal activities. He told me all this without a trace of cynicism.

Nanook's back looked very small as he disappeared into the massive, official-looking building. Whaling is legal in Norway, but the international community condemns it. Did the government intend to claim that Nanook had killed the whale so that it could blame everything on Greenland? But then again, considering the way Eskimos had been sacrificed to global economics, even if one of them had killed a whale, briefly reviving a long-lost hunting tradition, he would probably not be charged with a serious crime. On the other hand, what if the police found out that Nanook had lied about his country of origin, and refused to believe he was really an Eskimo? What if he was sentenced to life in prison, mistaken for a native of a certain country that insisted on killing mammals in danger of extinction on the pretext of conducting marine research, whose people's sole remaining pleasure was boiling that mammal's flesh in hotpots along with mustard greens and enoki mushrooms, or deep frying it with heavy seasoning, or calling it "chirping tongue" and eating it raw, or as sushi, or tempura, or steak? If that happened, crushed with guilt, I would stay here, taking any kind of job to survive, and go see him in jail every day, I thought, my emotions running wild until I remembered that Nanook hadn't killed the whale, and found myself laughing through my tears.

Nora was naturally upset but even Akash looked pale as they paced up and down in front of the police station. I stood, then squatted down, then stood up again. Though it wasn't a cold day, I felt a chill around my shoulders, yet no matter how many times I wiped my forehead it was damp with sweat. Cloud after cloud floated across the sky, dragging white ropes behind.

After an hour, Nanook came out, his face expressionless. When from three directions we ran over to him, he suddenly thrust both hands in the air and, smiling like a dolphin, shouted, "I'm innocent!"

My meeting with Hiruko put a period at the end of the long spring dream of a sentence I'd been living until then. What followed should have been another sentence, unlike any I'd ever seen, but then again maybe it just wasn't a sentence really. Because no matter how far I went, the period never came. There must be languages with no punctuation for a full stop. Like a journey that never ends. Or a sentence that doesn't have a subject. A trip when you don't know who started out on it, or who keeps on going, traveling to some faraway country. I wanted to go to a place where adjectives have a past tense, and prepositions come at the end of the phrase.

I was glad I'd flown to Trier. And I was looking forward to going on to Oslo. Someday I hoped to pay my respects to Rome. But just when I'd set my mind free like a bird, watching it fly over oceans, through airports, to the top of a mountain peak, the sky suddenly went dark and I heard thunder rumbling. Or so I thought until I realized it was my telephone ringing.

"Won't you come have dinner with me tonight?" my mother pleaded from the shore beyond my phone. Already afraid I wouldn't be able to refuse, I was locked in hand-to-hand combat with my own wishy-washy self. Pressing on the top of my head to lower my voice I said, "I can't tonight. I have to catch a 6:15 flight for Oslo tomorrow morning," but without even noticing the change she continued her assault as if I were still a boy soprano.

"What will you do in Oslo?"

Suppressing waves of turmoil, I lowered my voice even further.

"Research," I answered

"What kind of research?"

"I'll tell you about it sometime. But I'm busy now so I've got to hang up—I'll call next week."

"Wait," she said just as I was about to cut her off. "Actually, I'm sick." Couldn't hang up now. Not that I was really worried—this probably wasn't anything new, just the same old ailment she's always had, but since it doesn't have a name, she has to tell me all about her symptoms every time.

She couldn't go out, either to shop or to go to a restaurant, so she hadn't eaten anything in three days.

"Why can't you go out?" I threw the shortest question I could think of straight at her, but she didn't answer it.

"Talking about gloomy things is so depressing," her voice said, sounding like the beginning of an endless spring shower, "but when it rains every day it's hard to be cheerful."

"There's nothing new about rain in Denmark," I casually remarked. That set her off—her voice suddenly turned nasty.

"So you've always been the Prince of Denmark, since the beginning of time?"

I had no idea what she was criticizing me for, which made it all the more upsetting.

"Could you be a little more specific?" I shot back. "You can't go out because it's raining? That can't be. Or do you have a boil on your face you don't want anyone to see?" Silence oozed from the phone.

There are two kinds of silence, wet and dry. Someday I want to study silence, its temperature and humidity, though I'm not sure it's a suitable topic for linguistic research. My mother's silence was now, slowly and steadily, boring into me.

"All right," I said when I couldn't stand it anymore. "I'll buy you some food at one of those groceries that stays open late and bring it over." This was not something I wanted to do. The shopping I didn't mind, but I was afraid that she wouldn't let me go when I took the stuff over.

I had to go to Oslo the next day, no matter what. I wanted to be there to hear Hiruko speak her native language for the first time in years. People say linguists live a long time, but even if I made it to a hundred a chance like that would only come once in a lifetime.

Tonight I wanted to forget about my mother and spend the evening alone, concentrating on tomorrow.

"You'll do my shopping for me? That's nice of you."

That spark of joy in my mother's voice made it impossible to back out.

When I opened her door with my key, lugging a bag full of Nordic salmon slices, a cabbage as big and heavy as a human head, thin-skinned little new potatoes, and shiny yellow lemons from the tropics, my mother came out from the living room. I didn't see any boils or blemishes; in fact her skin was perfectly smooth, her cheeks a healthy pink, and she looked pleased with herself, as if someone had just said nice things about her.

"Well, there's nothing wrong with your skin," I said, trying to sound sarcastic, "and you certainly haven't lost any weight."

"Come in and sit down," she said. I left my shopping bag in the kitchen and sank down into the living room sofa to face the person who'd given birth to me, feeling terribly uneasy: she looked as if she wasn't through giving birth. I wanted to stand up and go home, but if I ran away now all sorts of delusions would come chasing after me.

My mother said she didn't have the energy to go out these days. She had no appetite. She'd always watched television at meal times, but the week before, after just a few seconds of some roundtable discussion a sound came out like cloth ripping, the screen went black, and her TV hadn't said a word since. She couldn't eat alone without the TV talking to her.

"Call Yusuf and ask him to fix it then."

"I don't like talking to people I don't know."

"But you've known Yusuf for over twenty years. He fixed the fan in the kitchen and the washing machine; if you call him he'll come running, even just to change a light bulb. Why, he's practically family."

"You are my only family." It shocked me to hear her say that. "Besides, I can't sleep. I've tried meditating, or taking a bath, or sitting on the sofa listening to music before I go to bed, but I'm still wide awake, as if there's a chandelier on in my head even after I turn off the light."

"Have you tried reading?"

"I read every day. But it just wakes me up all the more."

I was debating whether or not to suggest she go to the doctor when she beat me to it. "If I was depressed without knowing why I'd go to the doctor to see what the trouble was, but there's a reason for all this."

My mother's been paying some foreign student's tuition—a sort of charitable undertaking. Having a talent for languages, this student had finished his course in Danish ahead of schedule. As there was still time before the university term started, he'd said he wanted to travel around Europe, so she'd given him travel money.

My mother isn't repetitious, nor does she stick in lots of extra adjectives. So why do her explanations always feel so long and drawn out? I tried to listen patiently, swallowing to suppress my irritation. My father never listened to her, and I'd always been determined not to be like that, but those stinging nettles of his seemed to have taken root in me.

Length isn't the only problem. She'll get stuck on one part of the story, dragging it out so long I think I'm being suffocated.

That night the buildup about how brilliant this foreign student was went on way too long. "I think," the pitch of her voice rising, "he's going to study medicine," she finally concluded. She seems to think a lot more of doctors than linguists.

This remarkable young man had set out on a trip and was now missing. Though he'd contacted her regularly before he left, she hadn't heard from him since. When she tried calling him on his cell phone, she got a message saying the number had been disconnected. She contacted the police, but this student was neither a child nor a relation of hers, and besides, they couldn't start an investigation when they had no way of determining whether or not he was in Denmark.

"I'm sure he's just gotten busy and forgot to call. He's probably made new friends, maybe even found himself a girlfriend."

"But he's so innocent, someone might have tricked him."

"Innocent? You think all Eskimos are innocent? That's what I call prejudice. Sending money to an Eskimo won't bring the Great Danish Empire back, you know. Denmark's better off as a small country. We can leave size and greatness to the rest of the world."

Knowing this would only lead into our usual argument, I stopped there. My mother hung her head, looking depressed. There was no use waiting for her to snap out of it, so I went to the kitchen and started washing vegetables. I'd been planning to drop off the food I'd bought and leave right away, but now I'd driven myself into a corner and couldn't leave.

When I was a kid I never lost an argument with a friend, or let a war of words turn into a fist fight. I could control anyone with language, pouring a whole stream of words down onto the other person's head until he crumbled, giving up before he had the chance to get angry. I never did anything I didn't want to do because a teacher or friend asked me, but I wouldn't refuse, either. Gently but firmly, I turned down every unwanted request and then quietly closed the door behind me. My conversations always ended when I wanted them to. Talking to my mother, on the other hand, was like playing chess blindfolded; with her alone I never managed to get the upper hand.

When we'd finally finished dinner my mother insisted I take a jar of lingonberry jam with me, which lead to another argument, but I couldn't afford to stay any later so I gave up, put the fat jar of jam into the cloth bag she gave me, and set off through the drizzle on my bicycle. Relieved to have made it home, I was lying on the sofa hugging a cushion when the phone rang. It was my mother. She'd bought a ticket for Oslo on the same flight, she'd be going with me. Suppressing the impulse to slam the phone down on the floor, I coolly asked, "Do you have some business in Oslo?"

"An old friend of mine lives there so I thought I'd visit her. I've been promising to for years now but never had the chance. I won't get in the way of your research. But let's have dinner together in the evening."

"I won't be free for dinner. I didn't mention this before, but my girlfriend will be with me. So of course I'll be eating with her. Sorry."

This self-defense mechanism lie would I hope shock her, but she was completely unfazed.

"Well then, you can introduce me," she said, sounding absolutely thrilled. "I'll call again later." She hung up.

I gulped down a glass of tap water to steady my breathing. Tomorrow she'd call me again and again, asking where I was, wanting to have coffee with me, just half an hour or so. There was nothing to do but cancel my flight to Oslo. It was upsetting not to be able to see Hiruko and the others, but if my mother appeared when I was with my new friends, the whole scenario would be ruined.

When she came face to face with Tenzo, would Hiruko be stiff and formal, placing one word neatly on top of the next? Or would she talk to him like family or a close friend, in short I-don't-have-to-spell-it-out-for-you sentences? Would she give him her latest news as if she were catching up after a long gap? Or not having spoken her native language in such a long time, would its content have withered away? What sort of adjectives would she use, and which tense, past or present—there were so many things I wanted to know. Even if I didn't understand the meaning, just by being there, I'd feel plenty, watching—and interviewing Hiruko right after she'd finished talking to Tenzo would be completely different from hearing about it a month later.

Damn it, I really wanted to go to Oslo. But maybe I could get Akash to go in my place. I hadn't known him very long, or Nora either, but I had the feeling he'd be an excellent messenger. Nora's head would be too full of love for Tenzo for her to listen as carefully to his conversation with Hiruko as I would have.

I sent Akash a message. "My mother's sick so I can't go to Oslo. I wanted to go, and am furious that I can't. Could you go in my place? I'll get you a ticket." I texted instead of calling because I didn't want to tell him any more than that. He texted me back right away. "You're not coming? I am very disappointed." That gave me an idea. "I can transfer my ticket to your name. I'd be happy if you'd go as me," I texted, which was a lie. I had the feeling he'd refuse if I came right out and told him that my ticket would be canceled and I was paying for a new one. Just as I'd expected, he replied, "If that's the way it is I will fly to Oslo in your place. Thanks. I will report back to you on what happens there."

The following morning, while I was still in bed half-asleep, my mother called me on my cell phone from the airport.

"Where are you?" she asked. "Don't tell me you overslept."

The lie I'd thought of the night before slipped out easily.

"The flight was changed, so I took the one before. I'm already in Oslo."

"Is that so? Then wait for me at the Oslo Airport."

"I can't. I don't have the time. I have stuff to do for my research."

"Which hotel are you staying at?"

"The Hotel Siri."

I had no time to check whether there actually was a hotel by that name. But there are Victoria hotels all over the world, so why not a Hotel Siri in Scandinavia? After all, Siri is the Norse goddess of victory and beauty.

I was in Oslo but just happened to miss her—not a bad scenario. If I told her I'd called off the trip because I'd come down with the flu, she'd cancel her flight and rush over to take care of me. I hadn't planned to give her a fake hotel name, but if I didn't answer right away she'd get suspicious, and I was so afraid that I'd blurt out the name "Shinise Fuji" by mistake that I couldn't think straight.

"The connection's so bad I can hardly hear you, so I'm going to hang up now," I told her, and finally cut the electronic umbilical cord.

I sank down into the sofa cushions and turned on the TV to an art program. The commentator, speaking French, said that Hokusai's picture of carp swimming in a pool may have inspired Monet to start painting ponds. One of Monet's water lily paintings came on the screen, with subtitles that looked like mosquito larvae swimming in the water. I felt myself being drawn into that pond. The mosquito larvae floating on the surface didn't matter, nor did the fact that the TV screen was taller than the canvas. I was too lazy to go to an art museum, but Monet's spirit was reaching out to me through the TV. The more I thought about that the funnier it seemed.

Monet apparently collected over two hundred ukiyo-e prints.

Though this had nothing to do with me, I kept hearing a voice whisper from a forest somewhere in a corner of my brain, "Oh yes it does, yes it does."

The next picture was not a pond, but of the sea. A beach, with deep blue encroaching on white sand. A cape jutting out in the distance. Ah, the sea. I could hear the waves. The gritty wind, and sunlight so intense it makes your eyelids heavy. Nothing is actually one color, not the sky, the cape or the water—they're all a mixture of the colors in sunlight. How can all those countless colors be expressed in language? If I tried to say all their names in one long list, everyone would stop listening quite a while before I got to the end. Monet's colors change with each brushstroke, yet his landscapes appear as a whole. But the Monet on the program still wasn't satisfied. "This isn't right," he murmured. "It's not this sea."

"But isn't the sea at Pourville the one you've always wanted to paint?" the young man standing next to him asked, sounding concerned. He was dressed in blue jeans. This is not what a fin de siècle Frenchman would wear, so this narrator must have been someone from the present day who'd slipped back into Monet's time. The sea in the background turned into a sea from one of Monet's paintings.

The scene next switched to indoors, where Monet was staring at an ukiyo-e print. The brightness of the sky makes us feel lonely because it doesn't seem to need human beings.

"Is there such beauty in Europe?" Monet murmured. "If so, it can only be found in Scandinavia."

I think I know what he means. When I was in high school, I went alone to see the Mediterranean Sea one summer. It was pretty all right, but every scene looked like a painting I'd seen in some art museum. Are the pictures there first, and the scenery just imitations that come later? Afraid I'd get trapped in that artificial beauty, I rushed back to Scandinavia, and the next summer I went to the Lofoten Islands in Norway. Those mountain peaks soaring straight up to the sky seemed to be mocking human standards of beauty. *Homo sapiens,* they roared, *in your frailty you find beauty only in gentle slopes and green fields, in a mild climate, in calm seas and inlets where you can catch fish, in places where even weaklings like you can survive, in scenery with no value except as your home. You're so pleased with yourselves, singing the praises of what you call natural beauty. When in reality, nature takes no notice of your existence.* I was startled, but at the same time my body seemed to have become very light, almost transparent.

While I was daydreaming, lost in my thoughts, the scene on the TV had moved on to show Monet, now standing alone at a desolate train station, looking around, bewildered. "Monet has finally arrived in Christiana," the narrator said. Hearing the word "Christiana" I twisted around as I sat up, lost my balance, and almost fell off the sofa. "Christiana" was the Danish name for Oslo, still in use when Monet went there.

And now I was in Oslo, the city where Hiruko and the others were. Monet had taken me there while I was lying on the sofa.

Having arrived in Norway, Monet heaved a sigh. An oppressive layer of heavy snow covered the entire scene. "I came here hoping to see snow," whispered Monet, "but there's too much of it. I wanted to paint patches of leftover snow, not a whole blanket." Some might say he was being self-centered. Snow doesn't fall according to our plans, in just the right amount.

In the next scene Monet looked cold, rubbing his hands together as he painted the outline of a mountain. His easel, set up in the snow, tilted slightly to one side. The canvas was covered in yellowish snow, with a mountain shaped like a toad seen from behind. To the left of it was a hill, like a baby toad. A toad with a child in tow. Not exactly elegant, but appealing in a way. It must have suddenly got colder, because Monet hurriedly put his brushes and paints away and rushed into his wooden cabin. Once inside he set up his easel and took up his brush again. A woman with a shawl over her shoulders, her hair in a bun, came up behind him and said, "Oh, I see you're painting Mount Kolsass today."

"This isn't Mount Kolsass," Monet said gruffly. "It's Fuji."

"Fuji?" the woman repeated, looking puzzled. Monet closed his eyes and saw Hokusai's Fuji. There was snow on it. As it wasn't covered completely, the dark strips of earth stood out, rather like letters. Though the picture had no sense of depth or weight, the moisture in the air came through, somewhat cold yet ever so slightly warm.

Mt. Kolsass and Mt. Fuji don't look at all alike, I thought. They're as different as Finnish and Danish. But in both pictures, you feel someone's presence, face to face with the mountain. Not like they're seeing themselves in its shape: the mountain's so huge it could wipe them out. Standing there, facing it, they become aware of what's dark and heavy in themselves. A self they would never think of while daydreaming in a spring field.

The phone rang. It was my mother. I prepared myself for a tongue lashing, but she sounded cheerful.

"I'm in the hotel lobby now," she said. "It's very nice, but you haven't checked in yet, have you? Where are you now? And how's your work going?"

"Yeah, well, ah …"

"Remember, you're going to introduce me to your girlfriend tonight."

Cell phones always whisper, "Go ahead, lie," even to callers with nothing of the sort in mind. My mother didn't know I was lying here on the sofa watching TV. The fact that there actually was a Hotel Siri had given me a reprieve, but I still wanted to hang up as soon as possible.

"Well, I'm off to meet my friend now, but I'll call again later."

"Fine. I'm busy now, so I'll talk to you later," I said, concentrating on keeping the cracks out of my voice. When I hung up, I noticed I had a voicemail from Akash.

"How are you, Knut? And how is your mother? It's really too bad you couldn't come to Oslo. Everyone misses you. I found that restaurant called Shinise Fuji. I met Hiruko and Nora there, too. And we found Tenzo. But he is actually an Eskimo named Nanook. He wasn't lying about his country of origin. It's just that everyone around him, including Nora, came to their own mistaken conclusions about him. He really is a sushi chef, and it is also true that he is researching dashi. So if you think of Tenzo not as a false name, but as the stage name of someone selling the art of cooking, you can't be angry with him. He has quite a talent for languages, and has learned several. So he was able to speak to Hiruko in her lost language as well. She wasn't the least bit angry to find out that he was Nanook rather than Tenzo. She now says that the whole idea of 'native speaker' is rather childish. I suspect this will be of great interest to you."

I felt restless. I wanted to fly there right now. Tenzo is an Eskimo — that made things much more interesting. As did the fact that Hiruko was having doubts about the difference between native and non-native speakers.

I'd had my own doubts about the word "native" for some time now. Some people assume that the language of a native speaker is perfectly fused with her soul. And some still believe your native language is wired into your brain from the time you're born. Of course that's a myth you can't even dress up in the invisibility cloak of science anymore. There are people who think everything native speakers say must be grammatically correct, when all they're doing is faithfully copying the way most of the people around them talk, which isn't necessarily correct usage. Still others say a native has a better vocabulary. But most native speakers are too busy to think much about language, and tend to use the same words and phrases all the time, whereas non-natives, who move back and forth between two languages, are always looking for new words and expressions—so who's more likely to have a bigger vocabulary?

I wanted to see Hiruko, to talk to her about all these things. To hear her speak her language, in her own voice, right away. Why not call her on the phone, I thought, and ran straight into a wall. I didn't have her number.

I went back to the TV to see Monet, so gloomy and irritable before, now with a smile on his face, dressed in a suit. He seemed to be standing in a theater lobby. Like a frog who'd been carried off to some desert but was now back in his old marsh, Monet was lively and cheerful again.

"It was worth coming all this way to see one of Ibsen's plays," he said.

What's with this guy, a landscape painter who's happier at the theater than he is outdoors painting? I shouldn't be too critical, though. I don't even go to the theater, just sit here in front of the TV talking to myself about art and language.

When the show about Monet was over, suddenly the face of a political reporter I recognized came on in close-up, talking about a terrorist incident in Oslo. I couldn't believe my ears. So the rumors of terrorism in Oslo had been true after all. Scenes of a city corner, the camera shaking wildly. A deserted shopping district scattered with pieces of concrete from a building that had blown up; policemen hurrying across the foreground. Stretchers carrying the seriously wounded. A woman with her mouth wide open, a twisted oval. I couldn't hear the screams from here, or the quiet weeping. The reporter, strangely calm, said that the perpetrator had not been caught yet. Worried, I called Akash, but he didn't answer, so I left him a short message. "Heard about terrorism—has anyone been hurt?" Then I went back to the sofa, which no longer seemed like the right place to be.

I went out looking for I didn't know what. I saw fresh orchids and roses on display in front of a flower shop. Unlike the flowers Monet painted, the colors seemed sort of shy, holding back somehow. Flowers have a brightness you don't see until someone pulls it out for you. I went into a coffee shop and ordered coffee and an omelet. A porcelain rabbit was sitting next to a little Buddha on the window ledge like they were close friends. I wondered why Monet liked water lilies so much. Because he was attracted to Asian religion? The Buddhist god is a lot fatter than Christ but must not weigh much because he can sit on a lily pad without sinking to the bottom of the pond.

I closed my eyes and saw one of the ponds Monet painted. Deep green water lilies were floating there, perfectly flat. The trees behind the pond were reflected in the water. Both were on the same surface, but did they meet, or not? I saw the sky, too. Whether because it was far away, or very deep, it looked closer to purple than blue. In the bushes and at the base of the bridge, a tangle of flowers from purple to pink were in full bloom, showing off their colors.

I didn't even notice I'd forgotten my cell phone. Back home, I found that it had slipped quietly under the sofa. Just as I'd expected, Akash had left me a voicemail.

"There was a terrorist incident, but none of us were hurt. I am going to stay at the home of an acquaintance. Nanook says he will stay at the Shinise Fuji. Nora and Hiruko are staying at the same hostel. Tomorrow we are all going to meet again at the Shinise Fuji. Looking forward to the competition."

Akash seemed to be enjoying himself. I wondered what Hiruko thought of all these bystanders who had joined her. I was the first. Normally I'd have a hard time finding a reason to set out on a trip, but here I was, tagging along after her. The first time I heard Hiruko speak, the smooth surface of my native language broke apart, and I saw fragments of it glittering on her tongue.

The homemade language Hiruko spoke was like Monet's water lilies. The colors, shattered into pieces, were beautiful but painful.

I thought about traveling alone with Hiruko, just the two of us. Was that what I wanted? No, the others had never been in the way. In fact, without them we probably wouldn't have seen where we should go next. Tenzo had been just a name until we met Nora in Trier, where he turned into a real person as we listened to her talk about him. Because to her, he wasn't just a "native language machine," but her lover, the man she'd found injured, needing her care. Meeting Nora was what made us decide to go all the way to Norway so we could meet him in the flesh. Akash hadn't mentioned anything about how Nora felt when she found out that Tenzo was actually Nanook. Maybe he couldn't tell just from watching her. At least he'd given me some hints as to what Hiruko was thinking. But Akash himself I didn't understand at all. He wasn't just a bystander, and he certainly wasn't a nuisance either. Maybe he'd be like the column in the center of our group someday, with the rest of us gathered around, sticking to him like cotton candy.

The phone rang.

"I'll be free from about 7:00 this evening, so I want to take you and your girlfriend out to dinner. Someone told me about a really good fish restaurant, right by the water. You don't mind if I bring my friend, do you?"

My mother sounded excited. At top speed I rolled out the lie I'd prepared.

"After our last call, I realized I'd made a terrible mistake. I'd completely forgotten about this symposium today at the university. My professor called me, so I ran straight back to the Oslo Airport, and I've just arrived back in Copenhagen. I didn't make it to the symposium, but there's a dinner tonight I can go to. Some scholars have come all the way from America, so when I got the call I broke into a cold sweat."

"So you're not in Oslo?" My mother sounded flabbergasted. "You're back in Copenhagen?"

"That's right."

I heard what sounded like a sigh, but she didn't seem to doubt me, and I didn't feel the least bit guilty. What was with her anyway, thinking she could come along when I went abroad? Besides, this trip had really cheered her up. She'd been too depressed to go out shopping, and now here she was, jetting off to a foreign country.

After I hung up I went back to the sofa, thinking over what I'd heard from Akash like a cow chewing its cud. That sushi chef Nanook had taught himself Hiruko's native language. Not something just anyone could do. How well did he speak it? Maybe there was some similarity between Hiruko's native language and Eskimo languages. Even if they don't look alike, the languages may have some hidden structure in common that Nanook was able to grasp.

It was too late now, but I regretted never having studied Eskimo languages. Not that I wasn't interested, but knowing how thrilled my mother would be if I started researching Eskimo languages, maybe I'd been subconsciously avoiding them.

When I woke up the next morning blinding sunlight filled the room all the way up to the ceiling, so bright that for a minute I thought I was in the south of France. Actually, I'd fallen asleep on the living room sofa without even changing into my pajamas. I always slept in the bedroom with the curtains drawn so I never knew how light this room was in the morning. I didn't even look at my watch. Without bothering to shower I went out, just as I was.

I went into the first bakery I came to, bought some bread, ordered a coffee and drank it standing up. My cell phone was blinking, a message from Akash.

"The competition at Shinise Fuji was canceled. A dead whale

washed up on the beach, and it seemed Nanook might be arrested. Fortunately, the police said he was innocent. Something interesting: Nanook says there is someone in Arles who speaks the same language as Hiruko. So our next trip will be to Arles."

I had no idea how the discovery of the dead whale was connected to Nanook, the police, and the competition being canceled, but since he was innocent I probably didn't need to worry about it. What made me really happy was hearing that we'd be going on to Arles. My life had finally started moving and I couldn't stop now just because Tenzo turned out to be Nanook.

Certain my mother would call as soon as she got back from Oslo I was waiting with a program I'd thought up for the symposium I was supposed to have missed, along with the names of some American scholars, but the phone never rang.

Didn't I have a book of Monet's paintings somewhere? I looked for one on the bottom shelf of my bookcase where I kept the large-size books, like exhibition catalogs and photo collections. After sleeping a night, I had the feeling I'd seen Monet's painting of Mt. Kolsass somewhere before. I didn't remember going to a Monet exhibition, and he's not an artist I'm interested enough in to buy a book on his paintings. But it seemed to me now that I'd heard about him thinking of Mt. Fuji while he was painting Mt. Kolsass. I hadn't had that feeling the day before while I was watching TV. Sometimes the morning after you learn a new word you find your memory split in two, with one part remembering an encounter you had with that word long ago.

I once read about a strange theory that says there are very few words you actually meet for the first time, that most of the new words you learn you've actually come across somewhere before, and they've left tiny nicks in your brain. When you see a word again the nick is activated. So when you learn a language you shouldn't see it as something entirely new. You should tell yourself you're remembering a language you used to speak a long time ago.

I didn't have a volume of Monet's paintings, but I did notice a stack of magazines in front of the bookcase. They were all old ones I hadn't felt like reading but never got around to throwing out. The one on top was put out by a health insurance company, something I'd normally pitch without reading, but this was a special issue on the relationship between language and health so I'd kept it. The headline on the cover said: "Studying Foreign Languages in Old Age Reduces the Possibility of Getting Cancer by One-Fifth."

I also found an issue of the monthly bulletin some environmental organization puts out that my mother brings with her every time she visits. Though I tell her I don't want it, she insists on leaving them. "The article about dolphin language was very interesting," she'd said. "Dolphin language was all the rage a while back, but there hasn't been much done on it lately," I grumbled, "so I can't believe this article has anything new to say." Still, I couldn't very well tell her to take it back, so it ended up on the pile.

The headline suddenly caught my eye: "Dolphin and Whale Languages Destroyed—Deaths Reported." I scanned the article. Norway and the state of California in the USA were seeking out offshore oil deposits by emitting seismic blasts to the ocean floor that reflect information about what is buried below. These booms not only cause unbearable pain for dolphins and whales, but the frequency—every ten seconds, twenty-four hours a day—damages their hearing; one hundred thousand had been affected. These animals send each other information through their songs about where to find food. When they lose the ability to communicate, they can no longer survive.

There was even a footnote explaining that although biologically speaking the distinction between dolphins and whales is virtually meaningless, because the words whale and dolphin evoke different images culturally both were used in the article.

The message from Akash had said it looked like Nanook was going to be arrested after a dead whale washed up on the beach. Could there be some connection? To keep from getting flak from environmental groups they had to at least pretend to look for a murderer, so they tried to pin it on Nanook—was that it? Eskimos hunt whales, and a sushi chef might want to use raw whale meat—was that why they'd picked him? But surely the police wouldn't arrest an innocent person on the basis of such a stereotype. Oh yes they would—there were plenty of examples.

My longing to talk to Hiruko arose in my mind like a shiny black huge whale back suddenly appearing out of a wave on a calm sea. Since I didn't have her number I called Akash, and this time, he answered right away.

"Hey there, this is Knut. Thanks for all the reports, Akash."

"I'm so lonely without you. We've all decided to go to Arles next. Everyone's saying they'd like to leave on the last weekend of this month. What's your schedule like?"

"I can go. Of course I'll go. But is Hiruko with you now?"

"No, she isn't. She's gone back to Odense."

"How can I get in touch with her?"

"I've got her number at work. Would you like to hear it?"

"It doesn't really matter, but I might as well have it."

I lied. It did matter. I wrote the number down in pencil in my address book. But hadn't Hiruko already given me her phone number? There was no way I could have lost something that important. I had my cell phone set to immediately erase any record of my phone calls, so naturally I wouldn't have her number in my phone, but I was definitely writing this number in my address book for the first time.

When I called the number Akash had given me, I was told that Hiruko had taken the day off. She'd be stopping by in the evening to prepare for the next day's classes, though, so she might be there later, the voice added.

Though I didn't like the idea of making too many calls, I was determined not to miss this chance to talk to her, so I swallowed my pride and called once every forty minutes. The third time, Hiruko herself answered the phone. If she was surprised to get a call from me, I didn't hear it in her voice.

"knut, your mother, better health?"

"She seems to be over her illness. What I really want to hear about is Oslo."

"tenzo equals nanook. no native language speaker from native country. native speakers so ordinary, non-native speaker equals utopia."

"I wanted to hear your conversation with Nanook. But Nanook will be going to Arles, too, won't he? So I can listen to the two of you talking there."

"trier or arles, which one equals true rome?"

"Which one? I'm not really sure. Maybe the Roman Empire had the power to change any city into Rome. But I can't tell until I actually go there and see for myself. Someday I'd like to visit the real Rome. You know what they say—all roads lead to Rome. We're a band of zigzag travelers, going back and forth between Scandinavia and the Roman Empire. So how was Oslo? A waste of time?"

"travel to oslo my treasure. there mount fuji I found."

"Wow, does that mean Mt. Fuji is exiled in Norway?"

"different. two mount fujis. maybe three. maybe many more."

When was that? When did I stop getting old? Time passes by me like the wind. Maybe the cord that bound me to time broke when I lost my words. She threw me in Arles—I mean the woman I loved threw me over and then her lover threw me down on the ground and I got so sick of living I shut myself off from the world. Back then everyone I could call a friend was thousands of miles away, and "bonju" and "commontally-voo" was all the French I knew.

French words kept pouring into my ears until finally they started making sense, but when it was about time for a *bon* or *ça va* to come out my mouth, my lips and tongue just flapped around while the Buddha in my throat struggled and strained— I can't talk anymore, not at all?

That can't be, I thought, so I shut my eyes, pictured the faces of all my friends back in Fukui and Kiel and tried to call out, "How're you all doing?" But no. My mouth was wide open, but nothing. A sharp pain through the chest, but no sound.

I was *kozanikui* as a lad, that's "cheeky" in Fukui dialect. Unlike his mouthy son, Dad hardly talked at all. He was always alone in his workshop drawing diagrams and working with metal—cutting, bending, welding, polishing. As soon as I got home from school I'd run straight to the workshop to watch him. "Is this the robot's face?" I'd ask. "Doesn't it have eyes? What a funny-looking heart! Is this the switch that turns it on? When're you gonna put the legs on?" Question after question I'd ask, barely stopping to breathe. "Umm," was all he'd answer, from deep down in his throat, but I never thought he was being cold to me.

Mom wasn't home much, so when I wasn't watching Dad in the workshop, I'd be out playing baseball or soccer with my friends.

"This metal's got too damn hot," Dad was always saying. "Cool down." Even when a machine's moving smoothly, you can't let it get overheated. Sometimes when I'd be chattering away, so excited I couldn't stop, he'd put his fingers on the whorl of my hair and turn them in circles like he was putting in a screw, chanting, "Cool down, cool down." And when a robot was finished, he'd put the last screw in its head with that same circular motion. Except the poor robot didn't have a whorl, or even a single hair, which was what made them different from us, or so I thought at the time. Robots missed being human by just a hair? *Motsukene,* Dad said, that's "poor" in the Fukui dialect, so I said it too, "*Motuskene* robot." Then Dad scolded me. "You're going to Tokyo," he said, "so don't talk dialect." But why did I have to go to Tokyo?

"So is the word 'robot' dialect, too?" I asked him. "No, it's from Czechoslovakia." Don't know about the Slovakia part, but Czecho sounds like choco, so maybe their language is sweet like chocolate. If you made a machine out of chocolate, even the left-over shavings would be tasty. "Is Czechoslovakia farther away than Kyoto?" "Much farther."

Dad put a bunch of machine parts together to make the framework of a space station. Gears would turn, meshing with cog wheels, all going round and round. A shaft welded to a cog wheel would go up and down, pushing the wheel above it round and round. Energy flowed from one part to the next and, though I could see how everything moved, it was still so mysterious I never got tired of watching it.

One day, when he'd finished making a robot's mechanical

insides, Dad covered them with small metal plates. When you couldn't see the gears and things moving inside, the robot looked human. Then he painted a suntan on the outside, drew bushy eyebrows on the forehead with eyeballs underneath, dressed it in gray work clothes, and put rubber boots on its feet. "This is Kaku-san," Dad said, looking pleased with himself.

Kaku-san, whose inner workings were now completely hidden, shook his head from side to side, bobbed it up and down, and raised his hands in the air. When I could watch the gears those motions had looked really smooth, but as an imitation of a man, he was awfully awkward. Kaku-san was so clumsy I felt sorry for him. When Dad went to the toilet, I gave the poor robot a hug, rubbing his cheek against mine.

Dad told me that Kaku-san was modeled on a real person named Kakuzō Harada. The oldest son of a family of head fishermen, he was crazy about mechanics and technology, and always had to have the latest model laser fish-finder on his boat. In his midfifties, when he was hired by a local power company, he pulled up his fishing nets, sold his boat, and started wearing a necktie with a waves-and-fish-scale pattern. Dad didn't know exactly what he did at the power plant. Whatever it was, he was paid plenty, but just after using his earnings to build a huge mansion he got cancer and died. Dad's latest robot, modeled on Kakuzō, was going to a brand-new museum, where he'd tell the local children about how the area where they lived had developed, thanks to technology.

Dad always called the human body a "shell." As a lad I thought that since he made robots, a human body with no gears or other mechanical parts inside must have seemed to him like an empty shell.

Besides Kaku-san, Dad made lots of other simpler robots. An expert tuna fisherman, who stood up in a boat, let his line down in the water, and caught tuna one by one. Another fisherman, who stood on the beach, pulling his net in. These robots didn't speak, just repeated the same motions over and over again.

One day, I found a magazine lying on a table in Dad's workshop with a cover that looked to me like porn. Half-afraid of what I'd find, I very carefully leafed through the pages. Was I surprised to find out that the nurse on the cover with the sexy smile was actually a robot! The same magazine had pictures of a priest, a policeman, and a worker in a power plant, all looking like real people. They were not the latest models, but robots made long, long ago. The one called Priest No. 5 used to chant the Heart Sutra at funerals while beating on a fish-shaped wooden drum, and when he finished, turned and spoke to the mourners. It said in the magazine that the family of the deceased were especially moved by the way he lowered his eyes while he talked.

Before I knew it Dad was standing beside me, looking over my shoulder. I was afraid he'd scold me for looking at his magazine, but he was smiling down at me. "So, you've started reading technical magazines," he said. "Why don't you build robots like this?" I asked. "Like what?" "Robots that look like real people." "Robots should look like robots," he said. "Robots you can't tell from human beings are old-fashioned, and dangerous besides. I don't want innocent children to believe everything a robot says." "What do you mean?" "The things robots say aren't really words. They're mathematical formulas."

I knew Dad had made Kaku-san and the other robots on commission, but I couldn't see why anyone needed that new museum in the first place, and doubts stuck in my head like the numbers left over from a long division problem. The sign at the museum's construction site said it was to teach the next generation a history of their homeland they could be proud of.

Dad told me that when our town was a tiny fishing village, we used to catch fish you couldn't find in other places, delicacies we sold to high-class restaurants in Kyoto. Wasn't that a history we could be proud of? At school, our teacher told us the name "Fukui" meant a well of happiness that never ran dry, no matter how much joy you drew from it. So I couldn't understand why that well had gone dry, why there were no more fishermen. Would the museum solve that riddle for me?

Just after the museum opened, my primary school class took a trip to see it. Though Dad had always called it a museum, when we got there we saw the big sign at the entrance that said, "PR Center." When I looked closely, I saw the word "Homeland" in front, written in much smaller letters. So this was a "Homeland PR Center"? I really hated that "PR"—the feeling I'd somehow been tricked immediately put me in a bad mood. When we went inside, the first thing I saw was Kaku-san, sitting on a rock in front of a big screen with a picture of the sea on it. It gave me a ticklish sort of feeling, like someone from my family was there on display, so I pulled on Genta's sleeve and said proudly, "My Dad made that robot." He just nodded like he and everybody else knew that already. Since Dad was the only one around making robots, I guess that was only natural.

The sea on the screen gently swayed, and we heard the sound of waves. The plastic gulls hanging from the ceiling had tiny speakers hidden in their bellies. Somehow I felt the sea breeze on my skin and smelled the sea air, even though they weren't really there. Then, with a loud creak, Kaku-san moved his head and all the kids turned to look at him. A low, crackling sound came from the speaker in the pocket of his gray jacket.

"Hi there, kiddies. Glad you're here. Today I'm going to tell you how this town where you live developed. A long time ago, lots of fish were caught in the ocean around here. Watch these pals of mine do their work." I wished he wasn't trying so hard to sound young. It didn't sound right. But if he'd spoken the old fishermen's dialect, no kid would have understood him. We'd all be at sea, when no one was going out to sea anymore.

The fishermen at the back, throwing out their nets and reeling them in, were robots. Kaku-san was supposed to be the head fisherman, in charge of them all. But then why was he wearing the same gray work clothes Genta's father wore at the nuclear power plant? A shiver went down my spine. Could Dad have put that gray uniform on Kaku-san by mistake?

Luckily, I didn't need to worry about that because Kaku-san explained it himself. "There were times when we could catch fish, and times when we couldn't," he said. "Of course we farmed the land in the foothills, but you can't make much money from farming." When Kaku-san pointed to another screen over at the side, it lit up with a beautiful picture of paddy fields. I'd never really noticed those fields, but the curves along their edges looked pretty in the photograph. A bunch of little robots, each about twenty centimeters tall, started planting rice all at once, and for the first time everybody laughed. "We carefully planted the little land we had, and grew delicious rice." I was surprised to hear Kaku-san, the head fisherman, use the first-person pronoun "we." Then I remembered how mad the man in charge of writing Kaku-san's monologue sounded, arguing with Dad for hours when he came over to our house one time.

"After a long slump, our country's economy started to recover," Kaku-san went on, "but we were afraid our area would be left behind. Would we have to go to Tokyo to find jobs, as we used to long ago? We didn't want to live apart from our families. Just when we were all worried and confused, that nuclear power plant we'd almost forgotten about started up again. And it wasn't just one. Long ago, this area was called the Nuclear Power Plant Ginza. Can you imagine how happy we were?" As soon as Kaku-san finished talking, the Ode to Joy from Beethoven's Ninth came on full blast.

When I got home I ran straight to the workshop and said, "Dad, today my class went to the museum and saw Kaku-san.

Everybody thought he was really cool." That last bit I made up, because most of the kids were really turned off, and I was in a cold sweat the whole time. Dad didn't say anything, just went on polishing the metal rod in his hand.

The spring I started junior high school, Mom left us, carrying just an umbrella. But even before that, she was hardly ever at home, so almost every night I cooked rice for Dad and me, grilled our fish and boiled our shiitake mushrooms and bamboo shoots, and even took to making pickles. When I heard Mom would never be coming back, I felt like my blood was draining away, and my flesh grew cold and hard. But I didn't cry.

Mom loved rhyming and wordplay, and sometimes when she came home at night in a good mood, she'd talk to me. If I was gloomy because I'd lost a soccer game, she'd cheer me up with something like, "Loser, schmoozer, go get 'em, bruiser!" or if I was pouty and teary-eyed, she'd say, "It's all pie in the sky so why even cry." What I loved most was hearing stories about the club where she worked. They had about thirty different kinds of booze, and the most expensive kinds of fish. Every night they had customers like this politician they say never took his sunglasses off, even in the bath, and a ghost writer for mystery novelists, and a sumo wrestler so huge he couldn't fit into the tiny toilet they had there, and the head of a big corporation who always brought along his female poodle, dressed up as a man even though she was just a dog. Mom said famous people from Tokyo or Kyoto were always escaping to Fukui for a night of drinking and carousing. She talked to all those people, comforting them, flattering them, telling them jokes—her words could have a guy whose company had just folded laughing in no time. So her profession was using words to manipulate people. Which might be why she also had a knack for hurting people with just a word or two. I was always nervous, afraid she'd say something really awful. Mom was very pretty, and kind of refined, so some of my classmates said they envied me, but I pined for their mothers. Genta's mom, for instance, was like a big female hippopotamus, staying by her kids, checking now and then to make sure they were eating enough, but never fussing over them, praising or scolding them too loud. But if a poacher came with a gun, she'd shield them with that big body of hers. Genta's mom never pulled fancy tricks with words to delight a crowd, never sent a kid running off in tears, or started wailing and carrying on so that her kids had to comfort her, or any dramatic stuff like that. Maybe that's it—Mom would have been happier living on a stage: everything she did was straight out of a play.

At the end of the school day I'd start wondering if Mom would be there when I got home, my heart so full I could hardly breathe. If she wasn't I'd feel let down, and if she was I'd worry about what kind of mood she was in. If she was in a bad mood I'd wish she wasn't there at all. Maybe she felt the same about me, because sometimes it seemed like she didn't want me around. "If only you hadn't been born," I heard her mutter more than once.

Even so, thinking she'd never come back made me miserable. I guess it showed in my face. Kids started bullying me like a stray puppy. The school bullies had left me alone until then, but one day after school three of them cornered me in an alley, crowding around, hitting and punching me while they yelled stuff like, "You're society's garbage can," or "Quit wearing shoes with holes in them to school," or "Grow up, you baby," and after that the same thing happened again and again. Luckily, the first three times or so my bruises were on my chest or ribs, places you can keep covered, so I didn't have to tell Dad I'd been beaten up.

But then one day some kid hit me in the face, and I got a black eye. Before he punched me, he screamed, "Quit showing off that handsome face, you stray mutt," which made me feel kind of proud of my looks. When I got home, instead of going to Dad's workshop, I went around to the trash heap out back, where I wet a towel with cold water and pressed it on my eye.

The trash heap was full of discarded parts and unfinished robots. One was a torso and head that got under my skin somehow. No face, just a smooth, round head with no hair, but its chest bulged a little. When I pressed the bulge with the palm of my hand, gently caressing it, I heard a short "Oo," from the robot. Pure joy. I took a magic marker out of my school bag and drew eyes on the face. When I'd added long, thick eyelashes, it really looked like a girl. I crept into Mom's room, left just as it was when she ran off, stole an old, worn-down lipstick from the drawer under her mirror, and carefully painted the lips on. I put a wig on her head. Maybe because she didn't have ears, or because her shoulders were small and thin as a child's, she was kind of funny-looking. But then again there was something clumsy about Mom, too, even though she was awful pretty. An awkward, mismatched woman can make a man lose his cool. That red lipstick really got to me.

Though my grades were good in junior high, I failed the entrance exam for high school. The minute I saw the test questions, I heard "Fail, fail," clanging in my head. Since I hadn't applied to an easier school I knew I could get into, I decided to wait a year and try again. When I told Dad, he didn't object. With Mom gone, he shut himself up in his metal world more and more, talking even less than before.

Around that time, I started to wonder if there was something wrong with me. Girls with soft thighs filled me with rage. I'd freeze when I saw a plump girl standing at a bus stop. The breeze would lift her short skirt to show her soft, flabby inner thighs — no bone or muscle, just quivering flesh. Seeing that made me want to do something cruel. One time, lost in visions so horrible they made even me want to turn away, I almost got hit by a passing motorcycle.

We went on a field trip to a folk art museum in Niigata by bus to learn about handicrafts one day. In that region they have a traditional kind of backstrap loom, where the weaver sits on the floor with cords around her back, moving her hips back and forth as she weaves. The eighty-year-old woman who was showing us how it works started out tiny and shriveled, but as her hips moved her skin smoothed out until, like a shape-shifting fox, she had turned into a young woman. Looking down, I could see her breasts beneath the collar of her kimono. As her body twisted and her breasts jiggled, little by little the loom started to tilt over to one side and I wondered how far it would go because it looked like the whole room was going to collapse. I was so scared I shut my eyes. With my eyes closed I saw threads, too many to count, wrapping themselves around the woman's hips, holding her in place. "Ah, ah," the woman moaned, her voice getting higher, dying the air a gaudy red, as every time she moved sharp needles pierced the soft flesh on her inner thighs. There weren't supposed to be needles on a loom, but this loom had now turned into a sewing machine. Yes, that's right—there was a sewing machine in Mom's room. Once she used it to make a blue bag for me to keep my gym shoes in. That was just after I started primary school. I was so happy, and then for some reason I pulled a terrible prank. I took the pelt of a dead sewer rat I'd skinned with a kitchen knife the day before and hidden in the garden, and put it right next to Mom's hand on the sewing machine. She screamed, and as she jumped up she caught her hand on the needle, breaking the skin.

I got the nickname Susanoo in cram school. One of our teachers tried to make himself popular by telling us interesting stories from the *Kojiki* (Records of Ancient Matters). In those days, entrance exams often had questions about the *Kojiki*, and the teacher said it used to be required reading in the ultranationalistic days of long ago. But, what with the Sun Goddess Amaterasu being the chief of all the gods while her younger brother Susanoo is pretty much a flop as a man, the *Kojiki* seems to put women above men, so I couldn't see why ultranationalists would like it so much. I was in the middle of asking the teacher about that when one of my friends piped up and said, "Can't think of anyone better for the role of that nasty kid brother than you. Why don't you give it a try?" His quip for some reason was a big hit with the class. The teacher laughed, too, and then told me to write out all the bad things Susanoo did as a homework assignment. At first I wondered if that sort of thing would really be on the exam, but when I started reading the *Kojiki*, I couldn't believe what I found there. For instance, there was this young weaver girl Amaterasu had ordered to make clothes to be presented to the gods, and Susanoo skinned a horse and threw it into the hut where she was weaving. Shocked, she jumped up, and the sharp end of the shuttle somehow went straight into her vagina, killing her. When she found out what he'd done, Amaterasu was so mad at her kid brother that she hid herself away. Without the sun the whole world went pitch black. That much I could understand—there must have been a total eclipse of the sun. But could the sharp end of a shuttle really get stuck into a girl's vagina? Wouldn't that be a sexual crime? Couldn't it be that actually Susanoo stuck his pointy dick into the goddess Amaterasu herself, and she was so shocked her personality split in two and the injured part of her turned into a weaver girl? Whatever really happened, I hated being called Susanoo, but everybody at the cram school kept on calling me that anyway.

Since airplanes seemed kind of interesting, I took the exam for a technical high school where lots of graduates went on to become certified pilots, but I didn't pass. The school where I ended up had a course in shipbuilding. Back then when natural resources were running out and only military planes were allowed to fly, ships were making a comeback. Not just for freight—traveling around the world on cruise ships was getting so popular that even after some cheap, poorly built ones that looked just like those luxury liners in old romantic movies sank in the Pacific Ocean people were still crazy about ships.

I was pretty sure I wouldn't flunk out even if I didn't study too hard. What worried me more were my strange sexual thoughts; in fact, I worked so hard at keeping them under control that it was starting to wear me out. Seeing a woman's soft flesh made me want to lash out and hurt her. The cool, metallic skin of a robot, on the other hand, was comforting, and made me feel like a calm, rational person. I told Dad I was making arty things for an art class I was taking so he'd let me have the parts from robots he'd thrown away, which I made into my own robots that I used on the sly for sexual pleasure. They didn't talk at all, though, which was a little disappointing.

Once a school boy, a distant relative of ours, came to stay and asked me to take him to the PR Center. As I said before, the official name was "Homeland PR Center," but nobody said the word "homeland"—it was too embarrassing. I'd been avoiding that place for years, but with this likable little lad begging me, "Please take me, please," I couldn't refuse. He was so proud of my dad and what he did that he'd nicknamed himself Bot, and was always saying that when he grew up he was going to make robots, too.

When I saw Kaku-san at the PR Center, I was surprised to hear his new monologue. He was still sitting on that same old rock, but what came out of his mouth was completely different from what I'd first heard him say long ago. They must have changed the recording in his pocket. "After the safety measures were carefully checked, over and over again," Kaku-san said, "the plant was restarted. Ever since, our homeland's economy has been stable." Staring straight at him, I asked, "How can you be so sure it's safe?" He didn't answer. "Kaku-san," I went on, "We go way back, to before you knew whether you were going to be a robot or a human being." Then that likable little Bot took my hand, saying, "Forget about this robot, c'mon let's go see that cute girl over there." There was a new exhibit toward the back. Not a robot, but a three-dimensional figure made by laser beams. A young girl, dancing in a red dress. The way her pure white thighs appeared every time the hem of her short skirt floated up really got on my nerves. "Hello there," she said in a voice so high it seemed to come straight out of the top of her head. "My name is Uran. My big brother says the energy he gets from me will keep him working for everyone again today!" she went on, then burst into song, slightly off-key. "You think of everyone's happiness, you're so cool."

A sign off to one side said, "If you ask Uran-chan a question, she will answer you," so I asked, "Where does Uran come from?"

She stopped singing and said, "My name is Uran. Nice to meet you."

"Where do you come from?" I asked, louder this time.

"I am a natural resource imported from America, Canada, Australia, and other countries where the political situation is stable."

"Isn't digging Uran out of the ground dangerous?"

"If you want to dig, shovels are on sale at your local hardware store."

"When raw Uran is exposed at digging sites, doesn't the wind sometimes blow it into rivers, contaminating the environment, and don't people working on the sites come down with cancer?"

"Your question is too long. Please make it shorter."

"Does Uran cause cancer?" I shouted.

"Here is a list of local doctors."

"You are cancer."

"Thank you for your concern."

"You are toxic."

"Try to relax, and get along with others."

"You are stupid," I screamed.

"I'll do my best to give better information from now on."

I must have looked kind of creepy to that likable little Bot, the way I kept yelling at Uran, because he started slapping me on the butt with the palms of his little hands, explaining what I already knew in his own words. "She's just a machine," he said, "It looks like she's talking, but really she's only spouting lies."

Why did I get so serious when I was talking to a machine? When I hardly said anything to real human beings. Dad was just the same. Did we talk to robots because we had nothing to say to real people?

When the ground had been leveled, along with the locals' anxiety, the nuclear power plants started up again, one by one. One Sunday when I was passing by City Hall, I saw a group of protesters out front, sitting under a flag with "No to Nuclear Restart" on it. My homeroom teacher, sitting in the middle, raised his right hand, waved, and called out, "Hey there!" He was a chemistry teacher we'd nicknamed Snow Crab. He never talked politics in class, just calmly told us about the half-lives of plutonium and cesium.

Thinking of Kaku-san tore my heart out. I liked machines, but from now on I didn't want to have anything to do with robots or power plants. No matter how carefully you made them, they'd still be used for trickery, to hurt people. I didn't want to send any more robots like that out into the world.

Boats were my future: it came to me one Sunday afternoon when I was down at the beach with a friend, smoking on the sly. "I've got it! I'm going to build ships," I blurted out, surprising my friend. "

Don't decide your future in the middle of a cigarette," he laughed. "So anyway, which university are you going to try for?"

"Hokkaido," I replied, because Dad had just told me that he'd heard that was where Mom was now.

Kiel though started to seem better than Hokkaido after I met a certain German girl. Her name was Miss Hammer, and she came to teach English conversation at our high school for a semester. She was from Kiel, but she'd gone to university in

America, and had just finished a year in a training program with some company in Osaka. I could hardly speak English at all. Grammar was a cinch—I could explain what the conditional was, or the past perfect tense, but when Miss Hammer asked what my hobby was, all I could manage was one word—"fishing." When she heard that, Miss Hammer looked worried, and said something in English I couldn't understand. I did catch the word "nuclear," though, so I figured she was asking if it was really okay to catch fish in contaminated waters. After that, I started to like conversations that I only half understood.

Strange, though, when you think about it. I mean, if a girl in my class had asked what my hobby was, I'd be so afraid she'd look down on me that I'd end up saying something like, "A hobby? You gotta be kidding. I'm not an old man, you know." But when Miss Hammer asked me the same question, all I could think about was how bad my English was, so managing to get even one word out was deeply satisfying. Who'd have thought such a simple conversation could be so much fun?

In the next class, she asked us what we wanted to do in the future, and maybe because they didn't know many English words, my classmates all said stuff like, "I want to be an engineer," or "I want to be a businessman," but I wanted to answer honestly, so I said, "Making ship." I don't think it was only my bad pronunciation that made it hard for her to understand; maybe she took "ship" for the end of a word like friendship, or kinship, or even skinship. There are lots of different kinds of ships. If I'd added an "s" to make it plural, or maybe put an article like "a" or "the" in front, that might have helped. Anyway, when she finally figured out that I was interested in shipbuilding, Miss Hammer's face lit up, and she told me that Kiel University, in her hometown, was famous for its course in shipbuilding. From that time on, I somehow started understanding more and more of what she said. The week after that, I managed to tell her in English that my father made robots, and that I'd never liked the PR Center.

I wanted to tell Miss Hammer all kinds of things about Fukui. One of the hardest things to explain was how junior high school kids use the words *iiza* and *nayza* in Fukui dialect to help them remember the English words "either" and "neither." The whole class looked a little shocked when I pulled that off. But I was more surprised than anyone. Until then I'd never liked languages much, and hadn't ever gotten a good grade in English. From around that time, big changes started going on in my brain. The main passageway in there had been like a drainage ditch full of garbage, but a rainstorm had washed it out, and where the trash used to be a cool mountain spring now flowed, trickling into all the little narrow cracks around it.

Miss Hammer's face was smooth as a mannequin. It never crinkled up like the women in our village, even when she laughed. Maybe she had a firm bone structure. Her skin looked cold and firm, like her temperature was lower than normal.

When I picked up a pamphlet about studying abroad at a meeting about college entrance exams, my heart started thumping, my intestines began to churn, and suddenly I wanted to take a dump. Miss Hammer must have told my homeroom teacher about me, because a little while later, a pamphlet came in the mail from Kiel University. It said there were scholarships for foreign students. When I screwed up my courage and told Dad, his face crinkled up in a smile. "That's good," he said. "My work hasn't done anything for the world. Whatever you do, don't make robots."

"What do you mean, you haven't done anything for the world?" I asked.

"Remember that robot at the PR Center?"

"Kaku-san? Sure I remember him."

"What Kaku-san's been telling the kids is all lies. He's a robot, so he can lie all he wants."

People used to go abroad by airplane a long time ago, but I loved ships so much I never fancied flying at all. The ocean liner I boarded at Niigata stopped at Shanghai, Hong Kong, Singapore, and I could hardly sleep the night before we got to a port in India, where we were to stay for three days: the thought of walking on dry land again made me so excited. Yet after we'd gone through the Suez Canal, crossed the Mediterranean, and the ship finally pulled into Marseilles, I was so sad to leave my cabin that my tears made everything look blurry. There must be something wrong with me, not crying when Mom left, then getting all teary-eyed at leaving that ship behind.

I'd memorized only one French sentence, "Where is the station?" which I said over and over again until I finally got there, then after changing trains at Paris and Hamburg, I reached Kiel. Of course, no one had come to meet me. I managed to find the student dormitory by showing a paper with the address on it to people passing by. On the desk in my room I found a campus map, the orientation schedule, and some other stuff.

I worked so hard at figuring out where all the classrooms were and buying the textbooks I needed that by the time I was done, my whole personality had changed. I was now a simple young man who could be genuinely proud of having done all that. Kiel pushed my reset button, you might say. The boy I had been before, sort of perverse, always taking a twisted view of things, sure that someone was putting him down, had disappeared.

The intensive German course for foreign students started. I sat in on university classes, too. Just looking at the pictures in the textbook for, say, Introduction to Mechanical Engineering, I could get some idea of what it was about, but in my German class, the students from Scandinavia and Eastern Europe were already so far ahead I had to swim through this new language at top speed without even lifting my head up to breathe. Back at the dorm I gobbled up the sentences in the textbook and chewed on them until evening. I'd heard that if you chewed rice long enough it would get sweet and turn into sake, and the same's true for languages. And I never got a bellyache from trying to digest too much at once. In fact, I was high on my new language all though that first year. When people asked what my name was, I told them Susanoo.

There was a guy named Wolf in my seminar, and I always thought of him as *Okami,* our word for wolf. Anyway, one day after class he asked me if I liked the forest, and I said yes, but to tell the truth, I'd never really thought about liking it. "Let's go biking in the woods," he said. I told him I didn't have a bike, so he got me a used one, a mountain bike. Back in Fukui bike rides weren't for enjoying nature. The mountains were a good place to take a girl for a drive, or to sit around with friends listening to music while you smoked and drank beer, but nature wasn't something you went to see.

Wolf and I rode our mountain bikes on bumpy paths through the forest, stripped naked to splash our way, whooping and hollering, into the icy Baltic Sea, or played at fishing, never minding when we didn't catch anything, and then we'd stop at a farmhouse on the way home to buy sausages to take over to a friend of Wolf's to grill in his yard. Before I knew it, whenever I opened my mouth German came pouring out.

My major being what it was, there were only a few girls in my university classes. After seeing them every day for a while, I started really looking at their faces. Not a single one of them wore a skirt to class. There was one, named Anke, small but sure of herself, who was always looking over at me, so I decided to try talking to her. After just a short conversation she asked me out for a coffee, then to a movie, and before I knew it our lips were touching, our underwear was off, and in no time she was my girlfriend.

In high school I was afraid there was something really strange about me, but after I met Anke I started to seem normal, like everybody else. Maybe that was because of the hormones coursing through my body. If robots had liquids flowing through them instead of electric currents, I'm sure they'd evolve. Anyway, before I knew it I'd turned into a young man who loved nature, enjoyed talking to people, was good at languages, and could ask a girl, "You wanna do it tonight?" without missing a beat.

Anke was from Husum, so she lived alone in Kiel. One Sunday she asked me to make her some gyoza dumplings and miso soup. She held the soup in her mouth a while before slowly, carefully swallowing, then with her eyes closed and her nose pointed at the ceiling said, "Really nice," in a sexy sounding voice. She chomped down on the gyoza next, but must have found the skin kind of rubbery, because she looked a little confused as she chewed, but when she tasted the juice from the filling her cheeks loosened into a smile. "This looks like pudding but tastes like fish," she said, looking puzzled after trying the chawanmushi, then gobbled down all the green pepper and carrot tempura in one go. And after eating my sushi roll, she confidently announced, "This is the food of the future." She invited her girlfriends over for a sushi party to show off my skill as a chef.

I was used to fixing dinner since Mom was hardly ever home, but I don't remember it being much fun. In fact, I sometimes felt miserable, wondering why other kids' mothers cooked up tasty things for them while I had to do it alone. Mom just laughed and said, "Night birds fly away before the evening meal."

Dad never praised my cooking or complained about it, either. So I always thought cooking was like putting on your socks, say, or opening a window—nothing special. But now that I had a girlfriend I realized that if you fed a woman good food she'd be yours forever, and was kind of upset with Dad for not telling me something so important. When Anke enthusiastically applauded the meals I fixed for her, I bowed like a soloist at a concert.

Wolf liked my sushi rolls, too. "Great!" he'd say every time I made him a new kind. We caught fishing fever, got saltwater licenses and set out on the Baltic Sea in search of gleaming scales. I stopped spending hours poring over blueprints for boats, because it was a lot more fun to board one myself and go out to sea. Maybe I wasn't cut out for shipbuilding, or for university life, either. I hinted at that in a letter to Dad, but got no answer. Whether I sent him letters by post or email over the airwaves, the result was the same. I never heard from the friends I'd spent all those sweaty years in high school with, either. They must have forgotten me. I decided that from now on Wolf and Anke would be my family, and, uncoiling the rope that tied me to my old life, I left it on the shore while I boldly set sail for the future.

"I'm sure they haven't forgotten you," Anke said, "Maybe there's been some disaster in your country, and they can't contact you." She was trying to comfort me but her words had the opposite effect, digging deep into my hidden anxieties until finally I snapped. "Stop talking about that," I said angrily

I still hadn't decided whether or not to quit the university, so I applied for another year of scholarship money, but I'd skipped so many classes that they turned me down. During winter vacation I got a part-time job handing out fliers for a moving company, but didn't earn enough to dig my bank balance out of the deep hole it was in. If I didn't find a better paying job I could do while studying, I wouldn't be able to graduate. I talked to Wolf, who'd been managing since he started at university without either a scholarship or funds from his parents, and he said, "I can help you find a part-time job, but why don't we go into business together and make lots of money instead?" I guess he'd been planning this for quite some time. "We'll start a sushi shop," he said. "My uncle in Husum had a restaurant, but he died recently, and I've inherited the place from him."

Anke was happy to move to Husum, since her family lived

there. With the money we got from her father, the old, rundown restaurant was soon transformed into a trendy sushi bar.

The new Sushi Bar sign out front was unusual enough to attract customers, who were relieved to find they could also order the pork dishes they were used to, so our restaurant got off to a good start. Around this time, I gave up shipbuilding—I began making a home with Anke, who was pregnant, and worked hard at improving my skill as a chef. With no sushi training, I relied on books to learn how to roll and squeeze little balls of rice, and I'm sure some of the blunders I made would have shocked a real professional. But my customers had never eaten sushi before and didn't know enough to complain. I soon got used to life in Husum.

Things were going along fine until one day one of our regulars told me about a big demonstration in town. I checked the newspaper and found an article about an Andalusian matador who was coming to fight a bull in the soccer stadium and the group of environmentalists who were planning a large-scale protest against such cruelty to animals. The protesters would be arriving on a fleet of buses from Hamburg.

For some reason I suddenly wanted to see this bullfight, so I got tickets for Wolf and me. On the day of the fight, the whole town was seething from early morning, and the streets near the stadium were so crowded you could hardly move.

I must have been awfully excited when we got into the stadium, because I kept seeing little lights go off like fireworks, and I was breathing so hard I almost fainted and had to pull myself together several times. "I didn't know you were so crazy about bullfighting," whispered Wolf, sitting beside me, "We wouldn't have butter or cheese without cows, you know. Such an important animal, and they kill it for sport. Me, I don't like it at all." He looked very glum. And he definitely had a point. Blushing with shame, I turned away. In my mind I saw the bull lower its head, charge the matador, and stab him in the thigh with one of his horns. So that was it—I had come here to watch the bull kill the matador. That way, the matador living inside me would die, too. With him alive, even if I married Anke there was no telling what he would do to her, or to our unborn child.

These thoughts were going through my head when a woman in a bright red dress, her back perfectly straight, walked right in front of me. Her skin was pure white, and her black hair fell in curls over her shoulders. She was the very image of that female robot I had breathed life into when I was a boy. If I let her go, I might never see her again. I told Wolf I was going to the toilet and followed after her. Though her dress was long and she was wearing high heels, she was unbelievably fast. Parting the crowd like a swimmer, I hurried so as not to lose sight of that red silk and those dark curls. For a minute she seemed to be looking for someone, but then headed straight for the exit. When a crowd of people rushed toward me I almost lost her, but racing blindly out the exit and around the corner, I ran straight into her and we both fell down on the ground.

She seemed to have sprained her ankle. I helped her onto a bench and sat down next to her. She told me in English that she was a dancer from Arles, and the week before had been dancing every night in a bar in Husum, but was now on her way home. Her stage name was Carmen. I begged her to tell me her address, and with a sticky, sexy sort of smile, she recited it for me. As I had nothing to write with, I put all my effort into memorizing it. There was nothing wrong with her ankle after all.

From that day on, I walked around in a daze, as if I had a high fever. Anke started to look like a dull, boring woman. Her having my child, making me a father now seemed like a nuisance: it didn't make me happy at all. Why had Mom gone off and left me? Unless I found the answer to that question, marriage to Anke, and the birth of my child would mean nothing. I had to go after Carmen. I wanted to hold her close. If she were a robot made just for me, her body would be cold and metallic, and that's how I wanted her to be.

I was obsessed with visions of Carmen. Every morning when I opened my eyes, I saw the letters of her name. I would whisk those letters away and turn on the water to wash my face, but then I'd see Carmen's face in the gushing stream and forget about washing. I saw Carmen in the toothpaste, in the stream rising from a cup of hot tea, in the strawberry jam I spread on my bread. It was like a sickness. Once when I was sitting around, lost in thought, I realized that the flame from my lighter was about to burn my sleeve, and quickly put it out. Wolf asked me if something was bothering me, but I could hardly tell him I was about to leave Anke and move to Arles.

One evening I was wandering down the road when I saw a big truck with French license plates. I noticed it because of the two robot mascots attached to the roof. The driver was at the kiosk on the corner buying a pack of cigarettes. I made up my mind, and asked him in English, "If you're going to France, can you give me a ride?" He immediately nodded. As soon as we were off, I found out why. This driver loved to talk, and wanted someone to listen to him. He started off in French, but when I told him in English that I didn't understand French, he switched to English, sending out word after word to crackle in the air like fireworks with nothing in between to connect them. After a while he went back to French. This time, I didn't ask him to switch to English. I thought it would be enough to nod now and then, but when I didn't react after he'd told me about some seemingly dramatic episode in his life he grabbed my arm and shook it, saying what must have been something like, "Bet that story gave you a turn," over and over again. "Yeah," I said, "I'm really shocked," and still in shock, I fell asleep.

By the time we got to Paris the rhythm of that driver's French was so firmly ground into my brain that even after I got out of the truck I kept hearing it, just the rhythm without any content. I guess he must have talked all night. Maybe the patterns carved into my brain that night laid the groundwork for the French I learned later.

I kept hitching rides until I somehow got to Arles, where I showed people the paper with Carmen's address and, without understanding what they said, kept going in whichever direction they pointed. Those pointing fingers eventually led me to the edge of town, where there weren't many houses, and no one to ask for directions. It was already evening but the sunlight was still pouring down, making the crumbling white walls look kind of pretty. What looked like green snakes slithered across the tops of those walls, with red roses blooming all along them; when I found a house with the number Carmen had told me, I went through the gate into the garden where I saw a big man in a black hat, sitting on a stone by the entrance smoking a cigarette. "I'm looking for Carmen," or "I want to see Carmen," was what I wanted to say, but after I said her name, in a hot, feverish sort of way, the words stopped coming. The man snorted loudly, got up, grabbed me by the collar, and lifted me off the ground. Dangling there, my toes barely touching the ground, I let out a moan, and the man threw me down on the ground. Just then, the front door opened, and Carmen came out. When she saw me her nostrils flared, and sparkling laughter came from those bright red lips. I had been longing for the cold face of a robot, but Carmen's was now twisted into a mixture of shame, hope, surprise, and pity. Suddenly, she disgusted me. A condescending smile on her lips, she was now explaining something to the man. No sooner had she finished than I saw his eyebrows rise, and the soles of his shoes began to pound down on me. He stomped on my chest and my stomach, and then everything went black.

I woke up in a hospital. The nurses' whispering sounded like the rustling of autumn leaves. The doctor, handsome as a movie star, must have had plenty of confidence, judging from the way he worked on my body without saying a word to me, fixing me up like an expert mechanic repairing a machine. When I got out of the hospital, nobody asked me for money. Maybe Carmen paid in secret.

Once outside of the hospital, I had nowhere to go in Arles, and since I didn't want to go back to Husum, I went into the first restaurant I saw, but they only understood about half of what I said in English, so I gestured until they finally understood that I was looking for a job, which they gave me, working in the kitchen. Much later I found out that this was a popular Balkan restaurant—I had nothing to do with the actual cooking. I unloaded produce trucks, hauling to the basement stacks of wooden boxes filled with tomatoes and yellow nets full of onions, washed dishes, scoured pots and pans, and, after the place closed, scrubbed the floor—in other words, whatever all poorly paid laborers from a different continent do.

I worked in silence seven days a week, eating, sleeping, getting up and going to work again. Things went on this way for several months until one day the owner suddenly asked me if I knew how to make sushi. As I had no reason to lie, I nodded, and was taken by car to a brand-new restaurant on the other side of town. A childhood friend of the owner's had asked him to invest in a sushi bar he was starting up, but three days before they were due to open his sushi chef had run away. Customers had already made reservations, and they had invited people from the media as well, so they couldn't stay closed on opening night. They'd looked everywhere for a new sushi chef, but couldn't find one on such short notice. Until they finally found me that is.

Looking back, I remembered that when I got my job at the Balkan Restaurant they asked for a passport or driver's license, but instead I showed them an article from the local Husum

newspaper with a photo of me in our sushi bar. Maybe that had
stuck in the owner's mind.

This new sushi restaurant got popular fast, making the owner
very happy, and the guy from the Balkan restaurant was pleased
with himself for having found me, so my salary went way up, but
all those dry paper bills didn't make me happy at all—in fact,
I just stuck them into a plastic bag I kept under my mattress. I
had lost my voice, and that was depressing. I still had language.
I could understand what the people around me said. I heard
the voices of students working part-time when they stuck their
heads into the kitchen to call out, "Is there raw squid today?" or
"Isn't the chirashi ready yet?" or "I need two more bowls of miso
soup." And I'd picked up enough French while I was working at
the Balkan restaurant to understand them. But when I tried to
imitate the sounds and say the words myself, no sound came
out. My German had dried up, too.

People accepted me as a guy with nothing to say. The customers never saw me anyway because I was always in the kitchen
sharpening knives, washing rice, slicing fish, cutting up cucumbers, or making sushi rolls. I'd be in the kitchen by around five
o'clock in the evening. I worked without a break until past mid-
night, then went home and turned on the old TV I'd picked out
of the trash. The reception so bad the screen always looked like
a sandstorm, which really didn't bother me because I just stared
at it until I got sleepy and finally nodded off with the light in my
room still on. I'd get up at about ten o'clock. After gulping down
some water, I'd go out, taking nothing with me. Maybe because
my job was making food for other people, I had no interest at all
in what I ate. I didn't keep any food in the room I rented, and
didn't have a pot or frying pan, either. It was enough, once I was
in the kitchen, to nibble like a bird on the butt end of cucumbers,
or odds and ends left over from sushi rolls. One time I heard a
customer say that in India there are monks who stay alive eating

only air. After that, I tried to breathe in as much air as I could when I was walking through the streets.

My favorite place in Arles was the ancient Roman outdoor theater. Its official name was "amphitheater," but my name for it was "the whirlpool of silence." Stone seats surrounded the round stage in waves that grew higher as you moved toward the back. Every time I looked at the empty stage I thought, "Good thing they don't put on shows here anymore." I didn't want to see slaves, their bulging muscles covered with armor, fighting lions. If I'd been born in ancient Rome, I probably would have been a slave myself. Or would I have been a stingy chef who ducked out of work to sneak in, dying to see a lion chew one of those slaves to bits?

I liked to climb up to the highest row of seats in the back and look down on the houses outside. They were simple, made by stacking stones, with bits falling off the front here and there, but in those square, solid shapes you could almost hear the builders saying, "These are real houses. Hundreds of years from now people will still be living in them."

The reddish roofs made the gray buildings seem warm somehow when I looked down on the town. Somewhere I had heard just the word for this color, a sort of dark orange with the pink of peaches mixed into it. Salmon-pink, peach-pink, brick-red, cod roe–red, tarako, tarakotta, terracotta. Sounded good. But no matter how good that reddish word sounded to me, it would never come out of my mouth.

I started down the sloping staircase toward the stage. The rows of seats, the passages between them, and the stage were all made of gray stone. While I was here I could never escape from gray, but a gray this soft and bright was much better than white.

That day, I saw a woman standing all by herself on the stage. With every step I took toward her, my heart beat faster. I'd once seen a picture of Mom when she was young. It was taken on her trip to Rome, at the Colosseum. The profile was similar. Not noticing me, the woman turned to the right and walked away. Not only her profile, but the back of her neck, the slope of her shoulders, the way she moved her arms, the shape of her legs— everything about her looked like Mom.

Had the mother who'd left me followed me all this way, to Arles? She must be pretty old by this time, so how come she looked so young? That reminded me of something my boss once said. "How old are you, anyway? That photo you showed me was taken years ago, but you haven't aged at all. You haven't managed to stop time, have you?"

That same day, a tall woman marched into the restaurant even though we weren't open yet. I pointed to the sign that said we opened at six o'clock, but she kept staring at me, then suddenly blurted out in German, "Does Susanoo work here? Or are you Susanoo?" No stranger had ever spoken to me like that, asking straight out if I was me, and it threw me for a loop; when I tried to nod, my head turned halfway around like a robot whose neck screws have come loose. If I still had a voice, I would definitely have said my name was Susanoo, but in my mind, it would be スサノオ in the katakana script. Now, for the first time it hit me that someone completely unrelated to katakana was calling my name, changing it from スサノオ to Susanoo.

"Sorry, I should have introduced myself," she went on. "My name is Nora. I heard about you from Nanook. You may not have heard of him, but surely you remember Wolf, the man you ran a sushi restaurant with in Husum a long time ago. His son took it over, and now his grandson runs it. Nanook used to work there, and after that he stayed with me for a while." As soon as she said Wolf's name, I saw his smiling face, and felt a pain like a screwdriver boring into my heart. If it kept turning, screws might come loose, opening a heavy iron door.

"You remember Wolf, don't you? We heard from Nanook that you were in Arles," she explained again. "Hiruko will tell you why we've come to see you. She hasn't arrived yet, though." German, a language I hadn't heard for a long time, pounded on the door of my heart. I didn't know how to open it. Lost in my own house, I couldn't get to the door. Why had Mom abandoned me and left home that way? I stood there confused, not speaking, but that didn't upset the German woman called Nora. "I don't mean to rush you," she said. "I know you're not open yet. Hiruko and Nanook will be here later. Akash and Knut should be coming, too. I'm going to the hotel to check in, but I'll be back." She went out the door without waiting for an answer. I'd understood everything she said in German. I hadn't lost my languages after all. Only my voice was gone.

But why were all these people coming to see me? I didn't know any of them. Nanook seemed to be a friend of Wolf's grandson, so who was Nora—Nanook's wife? Maybe Akash and Knut were their children. And Nora had mentioned someone else, too, a woman with a name that really took me back. What was it? Not tick, or flea, or fly, but the name of some other pest.

Just after I'd gone into the kitchen and set to work, I heard someone pounding on the door. I ignored it for a while, but the visitor didn't give up. When I finally gave in and opened the door, a young man who looked like he might be from India was standing there. For some reason he was dressed like a woman, wearing a red sari. Again I pointed to the sign that said we opened at six o'clock, but he just stared at me without blinking and asked in German, "Does Susanoo work here? Or are you Susanoo?" just as Nora had before. I nodded, and nodded again to his next question. "Has Nora been here?" When he asked, "Is Nora here now?" I shook my head. "Where is Nora?" he asked. I pointed outside, across the road, and as if he'd suddenly remembered something, the young man stretched out a hand with long, slender fingers and said, or rather almost sang, "Sorry, I should have introduced myself. My name is Akash."

CHAPTER 9   *Hiruko Speaks (Three)*

"*Anata.*"

The word just came out. It was the only one I thought of when I saw the man who opened the door for me. As soon as I'd said it, I felt uneasy, as if using a word I'd just learned for the first time. Who is *Anata* anyway?

The man opened his eyes wide as if he wanted a really good look at me, not in reaction to the word *Anata*, but genuinely surprised to see someone who looked like me.

Kimi came out next. This time there was a slight reaction. *Kimi* had touched his heart somehow. At least I thought it had.

"*Kimi*, I think I've seen you somewhere, *natsukashii*."

This word *natsukashii* seemed to be made of mist, a mist I was wandering through with unsteady steps. In Panska, I might have said something like "memories of the past are so delicious I want to eat them" instead. That seemed more fitting than *natsukashii*.

As he showed me into the restaurant, the man said nothing, not "Come right in" or "We're not open yet."

"You're Susanoo, aren't you?" I said. "I am Hiruko. We're meeting for the first time, but you seem like an old friend, someone I've known for a long time."

He neither answered nor walked away.

"Why don't you say something?" I asked and, immediately regretting the accusing tone, tried cover it up with humor. "There's an old song called 'I Want to Hear Your Voice.' Do you remember it?" Still no reaction, so to smooth over the awkward silence I tried various versions of the song's title, like I'm Longing to Hear Your Voice. That Voice of Yours I'm Dying to Hear. Let Me Hear Your Voice. Your Voice Is What I'd Love to Hear, I Only Want to Hear Your Voice, but they all missed the mark somehow. Susanoo watched me scramble, searching for words.

Suddenly I remembered Nanook the Eskimo. His pronunciation was so fresh and new. I remembered his way of saying, "*Ha-ji-me-mashite*": how the "ha" struck the air, how hot the "ji" sounded—more like "ju"—then how after that strong "ma," "shite" had slipped out all at once like going down a slide. I seemed to be hearing every word he said for the first time. When I found out we didn't share a mother tongue, I wasn't disappointed in the least. In fact, the whole idea of a mother tongue no longer seemed to matter; this meeting between two unique speaking beings was far more important.

If Nanook the Eskimo was a fake countryman, Susanoo, the man standing in front of me, was the real thing. He had no *natsukashii* words for me to bring back delicious memories, or even words that weren't *natsukashii*. I just wished he'd say something in any language. English would be fine. So would snake language. Hissing would be close enough to a word. Or if he'd caw like a crow. Caw is the first sound of "call" or "car," so it's already starting to mean something. But Susanoo wouldn't even turn into an animal. He just stood there like a rock, and I was a wave, crashing against it.

"You don't talk. You are silent. Have you decided not to say anything? I'm not trying to force you. I don't mean to criticize you, either. If someone asked me, 'Why do people have to talk, anyway?' I'm not sure how I would answer. But if your silence keeps on this way, don't you think it might lead to death? Imagine tens of thousands of people who never talk, living on an island. They have enough to eat and clothes to wear. They have games and porn, too. But without language, they decay and die."

There, I'd said it. I started blinking furiously. As if that would change everything, and I'd see a completely different Susanoo. But all I saw was the same silent man.

How old was he? Since there were no words to make his mouth move or his face crinkle up, his skin was perfectly smooth, but Nanook had said that Susanoo was a friend of the grandfather whose sushi restaurant he'd worked in. A man with that many growth rings in his trunk would surely be offended by a spring chicken like me using a friendly pronoun like *Kimi*. Realizing that something more formal would be better, I went back to using *Anata*.

"I heard from Nanook that *Anata* started a sushi restaurant with a friend in Germany."

He didn't react to the name Nanook. Now that I thought of it, Susanoo had probably never heard of Nanook. So we didn't even have an acquaintance in common.

"Anyway, let's sit down."

He twitched slightly at the word "sit," then reached for the back of a chair with his right hand and slowly lowered himself until his bottom hit the seat.

Sitting across from him, I felt more relaxed. I was so sure that finally talking to someone in my native language would be wonderful, that it *had* to be ... so maybe the pressure was making it impossible for us to talk. I shrugged my shoulders, moving them up and down then all around, telling myself to loosen up. A simple, everyday sort of conversation, like you'd have with someone in the dentist's waiting room—that's what I was aiming for. The words came out easily.

"Nanook tells me you come from Fukui Prefecture. A nice place, Fukui. I'm from Niigata. Nobody used the prefecture name, though—they all called it Hokuetsu. The old folks used to say the names of prefectures were all lies. Prefectures are like spare parts the nation can throw away if they break down, so we decided to stop belonging to a prefecture and be true Hokuetsu locals. How was it in your homeland? Do they still call it Fukui? Since the *fuku* of Fukui means happiness, maybe people were afraid that if they got rid of the prefecture name, they'd lose the happiness along with it. One part of the character for *fuku* (示) was originally a picture of the platform where they used to leave sacrifices for the gods. The other part, on the right, was a sake barrel. A long time ago people were always offering sake to the gods. *Miki*, they used to call it—do you remember that word? Like *kimi* only backwards. Sake for the gods. Oh, but this is a sushi restaurant, isn't it? So do you serve sake, too?"

That's the way. This reminded me of when I was in junior high school, the fun I used to have talking to my friends, seeing how far we could spin a conversation out. You got hold of a thread and just kept pulling it out, longer and longer. Not starting with something you wanted to say, just letting words lead to more words in an endless stream. Back then talking was so much fun we didn't need movies or computer games.

Susanoo still didn't say anything, but didn't seem put out, either. Sort of like a boy I remember from my class in junior high. A handsome boy who didn't talk much, but always used to sit near a group of girls, listening to them chatter. Maybe Susanoo was like that when he was a boy. He might be enjoying himself, sitting there listening to me. Just the thought made me even more relaxed, ready to move on, and I almost asked him about someone called Yatsushiro-san, how he was, and what he was up to these days. Not that I've ever met anyone by that name. As I said before, Susanoo and I didn't know anyone in common. Even so, I was dying to say, "Whatever happened to so-and-so? Is he still around?" and the name Yatsushiro-san fit the rhythm perfectly. If he said something like, "Well, I'd heard he was sick but when I saw him last week he seemed fine," I'd get that comforting sense of the past being connected to the present, not time continuing for all eternity, but at least for the last ten years or so. I could make up stories about Yatsushiro-san using key phrases like "school soccer team," "class reunion," "colleagues at work," or "wedding reception," but if I got too wrapped up in gossip about someone who didn't exist, the emptiness of it all might hit me with a bang. There was no Yatsushiro-san, or Yakuni-san, or Yatani-san, I could go on and on naming non-existent people, but where would that get me? Then, an image came into my mind, long legs, full breast, a beautiful long neck. Susanoo and I both knew her. Tsuru-san, the crane.

"Do you remember that story about the crane who got caught in a trap?" I asked. "And that good young man who freed her. He was so poor, and lived all alone. Barely managed to get by, working in other people's fields, getting a little grain in return, gathering fire wood or horse chestnuts. He was really surprised when a beautiful woman came to see him one day and asked him to marry her. After all, he had nothing, so why would any woman choose him? He was happy, of course, but when he accepted her proposal it never occurred to him that she was really a crane who had turned herself into a human being. It wasn't just foxes and tanuki—cranes could shape-shift, too. So could any other animal. Must have been a cultural thing in that part of the country. The crane hid herself in a back room and started weaving. She warned her husband never to look in on her while she was at work. Do you remember why? She turned herself back into a crane, and was plucking out her own feathers, one by one, to weave into beautiful cloth."

When I'd got that far into the story, Susanoo's shoulders twitched, and a sort of pleading look came into his eyes.

"What's wrong? Did I say something that hit a nerve?" I asked as calmly as if this were some research project, but Susanoo said nothing. I tried a series of words I thought might give me a hint: "Wound, crane, poor, young man, woman, marriage, loom."

On the word loom his whole body twitched.

"Is there something you remember about a loom?"

Susanoo kept pleading with his eyes, not looking as if he was trying to find the right words, but simply frightened.

"So the word loom brings something back to you."

That loom was gathering the threads of Susanoo's memory, weaving them together. I remembered seeing an old hand loom and an electric power loom on a field trip when I was a little girl, but I couldn't say how they worked. To me, they were both foreign objects, like objets d'art.

"And what about the crane?"

The word crane was apparently just a string of sounds to him, because he didn't react to it at all. The crane, craning her neck to see grain, purple waves of grain, or purple myrtle, or—yes!—a turtle. Turtle and crane, symbols of longevity. These two words weren't enough to bring back all those lost years, or a homeland that was now practically an illusion. But if language is a huge net, bigger than the Atlantic and the Pacific put together, then just by casting it in one place you could scoop everything up. If a crane didn't work, why not try catching a turtle?

"Do you remember the turtle? And another young man, also poor, living alone. One day that young man rescued a turtle from a gang of kids who were tormenting it on the beach."

Why is it that all the young men in folk tales are poor and live by themselves? There never seem to be any young women around. They eke out a living, tilling the poor soil, going deep into the mountains to look for firewood, or setting out to sea in rickety old boats even though they probably won't catch anything. When they sense the danger of not being able to reproduce, a switch turns on, and they start looking for a different species to have sex with. Maybe that's why a crane preening her feathers looks so sensual to them, or a ray reminds them of a naked dancing girl. Drunk on animal eroticism and so faint with hunger that they lose track of time, they wander into a different dimension. Perhaps Susanoo was lured to Arles by a female of another species.

"Turtle, the Ryūgū Palace, Urashima Taro, jeweled box."

Though he didn't react to any of these words, either, he seemed to be feeling my presence more strongly with every word I said.

"I came here to study, but I don't feel as if I've aged at all since I got here," I said. "I think it must be that when I came to Europe, I jumped outside of my own society and the time passing there. You know how people feel their age by comparing themselves with the people around them? How a woman will go to her sister's wedding and think it's her turn next, or when she's had a baby she'll feel like she's joined her mother's generation, or see at a class reunion how gray her classmates have gotten and suddenly feel old—well, none of that applies to me here in Europe. It must be the same for you. Living in Arles is probably like living under the sea, in the Ryūgū Palace. You have exotic women to dance for you, and you get all dreamy, smelling flowers you never knew existed, and drinking in the colors of foreign roof tiles, so you never get bored, but then one day you suddenly realize you're outside the current of time, and you want to go home."

I saw a slight quiver pass over Susanoo's face. My words seemed to be skimming across his memories.

"Do you have brothers and sisters? Have you heard from them lately? I haven't heard from my friends or family for a long time, and I'm afraid something terrible has happened. People in Denmark tell me to give up, and just accept that the whole archipelago has sunk into the ocean. But that can't be. So far I haven't met anyone who knows what's happened in my homeland. Maybe no one knows. I don't have to find out everything right away. If I just have someone to talk to, that will be enough. That's what I was thinking when I decided to come and see you."

This was a lie. I'd had another reason for wanting to meet Susanoo. At least, I'd given Knut and the others a different explanation when I'd told them why I wanted to come here. But now the lie sounded more like the truth.

Susanoo's head dropped like a puppet when the stick holding its head up breaks, then he peered up at me, blinking. He looked as if he wanted to say something. Now's the time, Susanoo, speak, speak! I wanted to pry his mouth open, not to shovel food in, but to let words out. Come, words, come, out of the mouth of Susanoo.

But his mouth stayed shut as he slowly sank back down into silence.

How long would it be before Knut got here? He and I didn't have even a fragment of the past in common, but we could still have a conversation. I'd throw out a word, which would land in the pond of his brain, sending out ripples until a frog jumped out and leapt over to my pond. When the frog landed, all the tiny fish that had been hiding in the water grasses would come darting out. While this was happening, so many things I wanted to say came to me all at once that I didn't know which to say first. I talk to Knut in my own homemade language, and though it's spontaneous and far from perfect, as the words stream along the wrinkles of my memory, picking up every sparkling thing, no matter how small, they take me to magical faraway places. Only Panska can take me there, not my native language.

What kind of a childhood did Susanoo have? If his parents didn't talk much, maybe he grew up without knowing the pleasure of talking.

"What kind of work did your honorable father do?"

Saying this honorific made me suddenly feel like somebody else. This was the Ryūgū Palace. Susanoo was a young man, and I was a girl. We didn't have names or addresses. The light outside the window was terribly bright. Sunlight you never see in Scandinavia, the color of a sweetly sour orange. We were standing on the stage of myth. Susanoo is an awfully strange name. Sullen, Smash 'em up Susanoo, a violent young man who made life hell for his sister, skinning a horse, then wearing the skin to surprise a young weaver so that she pierced her vagina with the sharp end of the spindle and died. Hiruko, the goddess with my name, was another, much older sister of Susanoo's. As the first child of Izanami and Izanagi, she should have been blessed, but since she didn't meet their standard for a healthy newborn, she was placed in a reed boat and set adrift in the ocean. Everyone assumes she immediately drowned, but maybe she sailed all the way to the continent where someone saved her. People say a weakling like Hiruko was born because the goddess Izanami spoke first, luring Izanagi into having sex with her. I'm a woman, too, but if I don't open my mouth the past will stay buried forever, and I won't be able to see what's ahead, either.

From the kitchen, someone called Susanoo's name. A boy with blue eyes and hair so black and frizzy it looked charred peeked out from behind the counter and said something in French. Susanoo nodded. Maybe this was the way things always were for him. He understood enough French to do his job, and gestured in reply. The people who worked with him probably thought he didn't talk because he couldn't speak French.

This is not the Ryūgū Palace, I thought, suddenly noticing the grime on the cream-colored walls, and how shiny the cheap red chairs were. Susanoo was a sushi chef. And I was a strange customer who had appeared before opening time to talk a lot of gibberish to him.

"I'm sorry to have barged in this way when you're so busy, just before opening time," I said. "But we are from the same archipelago, are we not? That's why I think we need to talk."

Susanoo didn't react at all. I tried the same question I'd asked before.

"What kind of work did your honorable father do?"

A formal expression like "your honorable father" was probably too cold to stimulate his memory. What did he call his father, anyway? I decided to ask him.

"There used to be lots of words besides 'honorable father.' Pa, pappy, pap, pop, pater, papa. Did you use any of those?"

No reaction. At this rate, I'd be better off trying to teach English to one of those little stone Buddhas by the side of the road. The language called the mother tongue is supposed to be perfect. I'd been hoping to meet someone who shared mine one day, and looked forward to chattering away, but now that hope was shriveling fast.

If he caught every word I threw him and tossed another back to me, we'd be able to fill in even the spaces between the words, like kids who start a snowball fight and end up making a big snowman, but this guy was so silent he might as well be mouthless. Of course he really did have a mouth, though. And teeth and a tongue.

If I worried too much about his not speaking I'd have a hard time talking myself, so I decided to pretend he was a friendly, talkative fellow and ask him another question.

"Did you come to Europe to be a sushi chef from the start? Or did you have some other *yaritaikoto*?"

I once heard that someone in a coma can hear everything their friends or family say to them, and sometimes it stimulates the brain and brings them out of it. I decided to stick with it, and keep on talking.

"*Yaritaikoto*—I'll bet that's a word that takes you back. It has a special ring to it. It's easy enough to translate it into a European language—in English it would be 'something you want to do'—but somehow it's different. Didn't *yaritaikoto* used to mean 'your self' sometimes? I mean, if someone asks 'What are you?' it's hard to answer, but when you find your *yaritaikoto* you feel as if you've found the answer to life. And if you don't find it, the people around you start worrying that maybe you'll wander down a dangerous path. When you were young, didn't your parents or friends ask you what you wanted to do with your life?"

I thought I saw Susanoo's cheeks twitch. My sixth sense told me that I'd found the mother lode, so wielding my words like a pickax, I kept pounding at what I thought was the right place.

"What're you doing, still fooling around," I shouted like an old man. "You're over thirty now, so you have to find your own path. What, exactly, do you want to do?" For the first time, Susanoo laughed. I almost stopped breathing. I had to dig his heart out of this mass of solid rock. Determined to find it, I kept pounding like a miner in the darkness.

"You don't have to follow in my footsteps. Carve out your own way. If your path takes you far away from here, that's fine. I may never see you again. But I'll be watching over you."

Susanoo's eyes shone wet with tears, and when I stopped talking, he leaned forward as if urging me on. My voice was now the voice of his father.

"Sorry I haven't kept in touch. But something terrible has happened here. If I told you exactly what you'd only worry, so I'll leave out the details, but I can't contact you from here. You're doing just fine—I can see that from here. When I say fine I don't mean that you're a great success, or that you've made a lot of money, or that you're famous, or anything like that."

Which part of my brain had I pulled this melodrama out of? It was embarrassing, but I couldn't stop now. I'd dug my way to the entrance of the mineshaft that was Susanoo.

"You're like a ship lost in a storm. You've lost your way in the middle of the ocean, and are fighting the wind and waves. It would have been easier to stay here in the village. But I'm sure you don't regret boarding that ship."

I had an endless stock of lines like this, so cheesy they stank like Limburger. But colorless, odorless lines would fall flat. And this story would have everyone in tears. Even though I had no one to cry with. Left alone in the ruins, I was picking up tiny fragments of a story and putting them into words for Susanoo. We two were the last survivors.

Feeling a tap on the shoulder I turned around and, before I even saw who it was, shouted, "Knut!" But instead of Knut, who I really wanted to see, Nanook was standing there. That was when I realized for the first time how oddly similar Knut and Nanook were, like brothers who don't look at all alike.

His hand still on my shoulder, as if to tell me I didn't need to get up, Nanook said, "Good afternoon. It has been a long time. Are you well?" A little too formal, but as these were lines he'd memorized from a textbook with not much chance to practice them in real life, it couldn't be helped. He then turned to Susanoo and said, "How do you do? My name is Nanook. I am very pleased to meet you."

Susanoo looked at Nanook. Then he looked back at me, comparing our faces. He seemed to be drawing gradually closer to my world. Stick with it, Urashima Taro, we're almost there. Ride the turtle of language home. But wait … did Urashima Taro really want to go home? He'd thought he wanted to when he was feeling lonely, but the place where he arrived wasn't where he'd wanted to go. What's more, when he opened that jeweled box, death, once so far away, came barreling toward him at breakneck speed. Why not stop struggling to get to that frightening place called "home," pulling Susanoo along with me, and start enjoying this entirely new space called "Nanook"?

"Nanook is from Greenland, but he speaks our language. He studied it by himself."

"I do not have a handle on your language yet," said Nanook, looking down, embarrassed. Handle—now that's a fun word, I thought. Couldn't you call those green leaves on top of a strawberry a handle? After all, that's what you pick them up by. You need a handle to pick up a language, too. But a woman with a handle on her head would be much too easy to pick up. Better not to have one, then.

"*Ai-en-ki-en*," said Nanook, stretching his hand out for Susanoo to shake as he looked over at me, wondering if this would get through to him. The Chinese characters 合縁奇縁 floated up before my eyes.

"People who are connected by an invisible thread are fated to meet, but the mystery of that thread is hard to grasp," I explained. But then I realized that what puzzled Susanoo was not the meaning of *ai-en-ki-en*, but my relationship to this young man who had suddenly appeared on the scene. "Nanook heard about you at the sushi bar where he was working," I added, "and told us all about you. If not for that *en*, we never would have met."

I was surprised at how easily *en* had slipped out, a word I never would have thought of using when I was speaking Panska. I didn't believe in some supernatural power that decides when two people are to meet, so *en* didn't even exist for me. If you use trite words like that too much without thinking, just because they're convenient, you end up letting the words control you. I was sure that speaking Panska was helping me escape those bonds of conventional wisdom. And yet here I was, using a word like *en* as if it were perfectly natural.

Nanook didn't seem at all hurt when Susanoo made no move to shake his hand; looking quite cheerful, he sat down and said, "*Kan-gai-mu-ryō*. I am filled with deep emotion."

I nearly burst out laughing. "That's a pretty heavy expression, don't you think?" I said. "But it really is a lot of fun to travel and meet new people. By the way, Nora's coming, isn't she?"

"She comes. She came."

"How is Nora, anyway?"

"*Jun-pū-man-pan*. Smooth sailing all the way."

"You bought yourself a new textbook, didn't you? You didn't use expressions like that before."

"*Kan-kon-sō-sai.* A guide for weddings and funerals."

"So your new textbook is a manual for writing speeches to give at weddings and funerals?"

"*Yon-mo-ji-juku-go.* Four character expressions"

"That's not a bad idea, using expressions written with four Chinese characters. That way you can cook up all kinds of content without having to memorize lots of nouns and verbs and complicated ways of putting them together, or how to conjugate verbs or which tense to use."

"But the expression *yon-mo-ji-juku-go* (四文字熟語)has five characters."

"You're right—it means 'four character expression' but isn't one itself."

As Susanoo lost interest, his head started to droop, so I peered over at him and said, "Nanook is studying dashi. That's what he's really interested in, even though he used to be a sushi chef."

Nanook took a deep breath and, as if reading a series of invisible words written in the air, said, "Homeland PR Center, robot, nuclear power, shipbuilding." As he listened, Susanoo's eyes opened into squares, and his upper lip rose to show his teeth.

"Nanook, where did those words come from?" I asked.

"Fukui. Susanoo was a child. PR for the nuclear power plant. Ships."

Still unable to grasp Nanook's meaning, I stared at Susanoo, hoping he'd start talking about his childhood. But it was like watching a flower wither just as it's about to bloom. I turned back to Nanook. "Tell me what you mean," I pleaded. "What PR Center? PR for what?" I guess Nanook couldn't get enough words together to explain himself in sentences, because he recited another series of four character expressions.

"Imminent danger, desperate struggle, TEPCO problem, empty arguments, vacillating officials."

Just then, though I didn't hear a sound behind me, much less my name being called, I turned around. Knut was standing there. I stood up so quickly I almost knocked the chair over and ran over to him. "knut!" I cried, throwing my arms around his thick torso, "waited, waited, waited." Gently untangling himself, he nodded with an embarrassed smile, then lifted his hand and waved to Nanook. He looked at Susanoo as if he were a bright, shiny object.

"susanoo. many native language words to him I gave," I explained in Panska. "reply to me he gives not."

Knut sat down in the last of the four chairs around the table, and spoke to Susanoo in English. "How do you do? My name is Knut. I'm a friend of Hiruko's, and we're traveling together. I came from Scandinavia to meet you. To learn more about your native language, and to find out what's happening in the country where that language is spoken."

I was so caught up in all the images I'd conjured up while talking to Susanoo that I had almost forgotten why I'd come here, so Knut's laying everything out clearly like a diplomat was a big help. "It was Hiruko here who wanted to meet you, and talk to you," he went on. "We are her supporters. Nanook, myself, and two others, Nora and Akash. I think they'll be here soon. I'm sure you can imagine how full of hope Hiruko is."

This time what Knut said worried me. It had never occurred to me that this man Susanoo I'd finally managed to track down with the help of four strangers wouldn't speak at all. Nora and Akash would be here soon. Then the curtain would come down on a silent comedy. Without some cheesy trick in the last scene, like some god floating down on an electric cloud and tapping Susanoo with his magic wand, making him suddenly start babbling away, we would all be left sitting silently around the table while the lights dimmed.

"What's wrong, Hiruko?" Knut asked. "Is something worrying you?" I placed my hand on top of his meaty hand, lying there on the table, and felt a little more calm.

"susanoo illness possible," I said in Panska. "loss of words."

"Hiruko says that you cannot speak," Knut said to Susanoo. "Is this true? Try saying something, anything. Any language will do." He sounded like a doctor. Susanoo was as silent as a fish. "If you can't speak," Knut went on, "it's nothing to be ashamed of. It can be treated, just like pneumonia. And there are many reasons for not being able to speak. In some cases, there's some damage to the vocal chords; while in others, a person can no longer find the words he or she needs; in still others, the person simply doesn't want to talk to other people. A friend of mine who works at a research institute in Stockholm is a specialist in this problem."

Nanook grinned and whispered in my ear, "Next we will go to Stockholm." I smiled along with him. This journey we'd started to find Susanoo had grown into something much bigger than that, and we couldn't let his silence just put an end to it.

Exactly at that moment, Knut and Nanook turned their heads in unison toward the door. With looks of surprise so much alike they could have been twins, they both let out an "Ah!" at the very same time. When I turned around, a beautiful Scandinavian woman was opening the door, about to come in. She looked to be in her midforties. She looked at Knut with a bright, confident smile, but when she saw Nanook, she must have been terribly shocked, because her lovely face turned pale before our eyes.

CHAPTER 10   *Knut Speaks (Three)*

I had a sinking feeling I'd told my mother I was going to Arles. I must have. There's no other way to explain her sudden appearance in this sushi restaurant. But I couldn't remember when I'd told her, or why. Whenever I talk to her on the phone, my tongue does a lot of twisting and turning. Like a snake that twists itself into an S to avoid a rock in its path, or maybe just out of habit. Ever since I was a kid I've been careful not to give my mother too much information. If I said, "I'm going over to Jens's house to play," she'd come back with, "That Jens—he has a sneaky laugh, like he's trying to hide something," planting doubts in my mind that cast a shadow over what should have been a fun afternoon. If I said, "We're all going skateboarding on the promenade to-morrow," she'd ruin everything by saying something like, "It'll probably rain tomorrow, so why not wait until the day after?" I'd ignore her, of course, but as soon as I got to the Havnegade big, teasing raindrops would starting hitting my cheeks. I was sure she didn't just listen to the weather forecast but had actually used magic to make it rain.

Now that I'm supposed to have left childhood behind, it's depressing to still be telling lies like, "I'm going to a conference in Nuremberg," when she asks where I'll be. If I tell her I'll be at home all week she might drop over when I'm least expect-ing her so I usually say I have a conference to go to, and with conferences on all the time somewhere or other there's almost no chance of her catching me out. People are always saying the humanities are dead so it's strange how many conferences there are.

If I say the conference is somewhere in Scandinavia or France my mother will probably announce that she's coming along. That's why one time I chose Nuremberg, which she believes is more permeated with Nazi history than anywhere else, even in Germany. When she asks what the conference is about, I string together a lot of English words like global transnational cross-cultural postcolonial bilingual translation to muddy the waters. But sometimes when I think my tongue is taking all the right curves, the snake lets down its guard and is so surprised when it runs straight into a rock that its tail flaps up for someone to grab. I don't know whether or not snakes have tails, but even if they don't that doesn't mean they can't be caught by the tail. I know now—Monet was the problem. I was sure he'd be a safe topic, but I never should have started talking about how he painted snowy scenes in Norway.

"I was watching this TV show about the life of Monet," I said. "The part about how he went to Norway was really interesting."

My mother says Impressionist paintings cheer her up. "Seeing a painting full of light makes me happier than going hiking in the sunlight," she said one time, "so how does my brain work, anyway?"

Taking that as my cue, I made up a theory for her on the spot: "The orange you see in a landscape painting is like a real natural orange turned into orange juice. It takes time and effort to peel an orange, chew the pulp, digest it, and turn it into energy. But because the painter has already done all that for you the color you see in the painting is like juice—you absorb it just by looking and it makes your blood sugar level rise."

When I come up with a really cool theory like that I feel like I can redirect my mother's thoughts just with words, which makes me really happy. Maybe it's coming back from that first thrill when I was a baby in diapers sucking on a bottle and then started talking and realized that even if I wasn't as strong as the grown-ups I could use words to make them do whatever I wanted. If I chirped, "Mozart!" someone would hurry over to a silver machine, turn on the switch, and play some music for me. If I called out, "Library!" my mother would put my sweater, hat, and boots on and take me to the library. When I screamed, "An accident!" she'd come running from the kitchen to look out the living room window, and if I yelled, "Something's burning!" she'd smell it and run back to the kitchen—it was so easy to keep these animals called grown-ups scurrying around.

Language, of course, was also a tool my mother could use to box me in, so I had to be careful. She was always nagging and I was always trying to get away, which was exhausting, so I looked for a topic she'd really go for, that she'd get so wrapped so up in it she'd forget about me. I thought Monet would be perfect, but that was a big mistake. The minute she heard his name, her voice went dark.

"I knew Monet came to Scandinavia to paint. But it was his pictures of the light in the south of France that made him famous. Scandinavia was just a distraction. Compared to Monet, you have to feel sorry for Van Gogh. He went to the south of France, too, but perhaps he shouldn't have. They say too much light can bring out hidden illnesses."

"You mean light can make you sick?"

"Well, in semidarkness you're connected to the people around you in a vague sort of way. You share things, like being poor, and tired from working hard all day. But in very bright light each person is alone—I am me and you are you. And when they look in the mirror, they have to ask themselves, 'Who am I?' That may be all right for people who can lose themselves in the light, but I keep getting darker, year by year."

"But you always looked forward to your trips to the south of France."

"Scandinavian winters are too long. I got so tired waiting for spring I always ended up going somewhere around the end of March. Montpelier, Aix-en-Provence, Marseille, Arles. That just made things worse, though, so I've decided not to go anymore."

"Good idea. I never want to go to bright, sunny places myself. I like quiet, gray, rainy days much better. So it's kind of strange that I'll be going to Arles soon—irony, you might say."

"You're going to Arles? To see the Roman ruins?"

"You've got to be kidding. I'm not some retiree with time on my hands, you know. I'm going on a research trip, studying a language that was thought to be lost. We thought there were no more native speakers until we got this report about someone living in Arles."

Having said this, I remembered that it wasn't actually the language that was lost but the country where it was spoken, but I didn't think I needed to explain that to my mother.

"Are you going alone?"

"No, with an international research team. Since all our members live in different cities and have jobs, working out a schedule that was good for everyone was a nightmare, but we finally settled on the last Saturday this month."

We were an odd group that had just happened to get together, but as soon as I called us an "International Research Team," it seemed to me that that's exactly what we were.

"Where will you be doing your research?"

"At the university."

This was a lie.

"No matter where you go you always end up at a university. Don't you get bored? Are linguists the only people you talk to?"

"It's fun drinking with people who are interested in the same field."

This was true.

"So you all go drinking together?"

"We're going to meet at the most popular sushi restaurant in

Arles. We'll eat, drink, and talk about language. You never get dragged into conversations about someone's divorce, or illness, or the furniture they just bought."

This was also true—all of it. My mother hadn't seemed particularly interested in the conference in Arles, so I'd heaved a sigh of relief and hung up the phone.

And until now, I'd completely forgotten about our conversation.

Hiruko, Nanook, Nora, Akash and I actually planned out our strategy for finding Susanoo pretty carefully, looking up the most popular sushi restaurant in Arles ahead of time and agreeing to meet there. We thought Susanoo might be working there, and even if he wasn't we could get more information from the people there, and were ready to check out all the sushi restaurants in Arles if we had to. It didn't occur to me that my mother could look up the most popular sushi restaurant in Arles just as easily as we had.

I left Hiruko, Susanoo, and Nanook sitting at the table and went over to the door where my mother was standing to hiss some accusations into her ear.

"You said you weren't going to the south of France anymore—so why are you in Arles? This is like being followed around by a private detective, and it doesn't feel very good."

To my surprise, she completely ignored me and marched straight over to the table where the others were sitting.

"What are you doing here? Why didn't you contact me? Where have you been all this time?" Nanook sat there looking down as she stared at him, pouring questions down on his jet black head in a quiet, ominously suppressed voice that seemed about to explode any minute.

How did my mother know Nanook? Fragments of memory were running a relay race in my brain, overtaking one another until finally the anchor yelled "A!" and crossed the finish line.

This "A," unlike any of the officially recognized phonetic sounds in the Danish language, sounded more like a crow than a human voice. The thought I might change into some creature unable to utter human sounds frightened me. Apparently shocked by my inhuman "A!" Hiruko shouted "E!" Though this was probably supposed to be just another interjection, there was a stickiness about the way she said it that suggested there was more to it. But this was no time to be parsing interjections. Forcing my way in front of my mother, who saw only Nanook, I said, "You told me you were sponsoring a brilliant foreign student, paying his tuition so he could study in Copenhagen. And that you'd stopped hearing from him after he left on a trip. Is that the young man Nanook here?"

Raising her eyebrows, Hiruko looked back and forth between my mother and Nanook. I was sure Susanoo didn't understand Danish. Expressionless, he sat there staring at a hole in the air, but I didn't feel like translating the conversation into English for him. I must have sounded like a crow to my mother, too, because she didn't react to what I'd said at all and kept on talking to Nanook.

"Why are you in Arles? What are you doing here? When are you coming back to Copenhagen? When are you going to the university?

Having asked Nanook all the questions she could think of, she pressed her lips together and waited for him to answer. The silence grew heavier. Just like another time I remember. I must have been about twelve. I was smoking hashish in my room when my mother suddenly burst in and asked in a deep throaty voice, "What's that smell?" then silently waited for an answer. I could tell she was ready to stand there until sunrise the next morning. I thought I was going to suffocate, and had a coughing fit. Though it was Nanook she was interrogating now, I felt like I had to say something, and sent my train of accusations down the usual track.

"Aren't you upset only because you think this young man from our former colony should be grateful to you for paying his tuition? But you were really only doing it for yourself. Your life was starting to seem meaningless, so you wanted to help someone, and hit on the idea of sponsoring a foreign student. But have you ever looked at things from Nanook's point of view? It's as if you bought him with that money. Lots of people start studying at university and then decide to go in a different direction. Are you saying he doesn't have that right?"

" But then why didn't he come out and tell me honestly what he wanted to do instead of just disappearing?" she said, staring at me as if I were Nanook. "He could at least explain himself to me."

"A guy can't open up to his sponsor about what's troubling him."

"Sponsor? I consider myself his surrogate mother."

"You think forking out money makes you a parent?"

"You're just jealous, because a doctor's actually useful."

"Remember that TV show we used to watch together, Lars von Trier's *The Kingdom*? How can you still respect doctors after seeing all the stuff that went on in that hospital?" I didn't have even the slightest idea why Nanook had started making sushi and researching dashi instead of going to university, and here I was making up a reason for him to give up on medicine.

My mother stood there a while, dumbfounded, taking in these last words, but then maybe because she'd suddenly realized that it was Knut saying them and not Nanook, she started shaking her head from side to side, so hard her hair got all messed up.

"If you know so much about Nanook," she finally said, "why didn't you let me know he was all right? I was so worried I couldn't sleep. And now I'm even sicker than I was before."

"I didn't know."

"You didn't know, and yet you agreed to meet him here in Arles?"

"I only knew him as a member of our research team. That's the truth."

"You mean that's the truth and everything else is a lie?"

Hiruko burst out laughing, and my mother threw her an accusing glance.

"Who are you?" she asked.

"hiruko. knut a man in love with language. i also language do love. same love we share."

Listening to Panska for the first time, my mother looked confused. For a second her brow was knit in consternation, then suddenly her whole face relaxed into a droopy-eyed smile. Her disdain for deviant language was at war with her protective feelings toward foreigners, leaving her badly shaken. As if I'd been watching a sign teetering back and forth in a strong wind and suddenly, out of sheer spite, had decided to push it over, I announced, "Hiruko is my lover."

My mother's face was perfectly still. Hiruko giggled and said, "such old concept is lover. side by side we two walk." Leave it to Hiruko. Side by side we two walk—nicely put. Unable to decide whether to speak to Hiruko or go back to interrogating Nanook, my mother's head swung back and forth, first to one and then to the other.

"Anyway, why don't you sit down?" I said.

I dragged over a chair from the next table for her, then sat down myself and saw that the extra chair ruined the perfect square Hiruko, Susanoo, Nanook and I had formed.

Putting that aside, this certainly was a strange meeting. I was sitting at a table with the person who'd given birth to me, my fake younger brother, my fake lover, and a countryman of hers. Having come here to observe Hiruko's conversation with Susanoo, who shared her native language, I had discovered that Susanoo could no longer speak any language, and we were now supposed to be discussing whether or not to take him to Stockholm to see if my friend who specializes in speech loss could cure him.

Then the focus had shifted to this problem between my mother and Nanook. Rattled by my mother's sudden appearance, I'd turned on the faucet and let a stream of useless discourse gush out, which was my fault. I mustn't take this so seriously. I had to loosen up, tell myself that this was all a game, and get things under control again. It was a game, all right, but with a lot more language than any computer game. More like a TV talk show. One where the panelists get all worked up about something that means nothing to all those people sitting in their living rooms enjoying themselves, watching them talk until they're red in the face, or about to burst into tears.

"All right, then," I said, pretending to be the moderator, "if you have any questions for Nanook, go ahead and ask."

Now that she'd officially been given permission to speak, my mother calmed down and started talking.

"After you finished your language course you said you were going to travel around Denmark until the new semester started. Why didn't you return from your trip?"

"I started working part-time in a sushi restaurant," Nanook said in a strained, weak voice. "That's what got me off the old path."

"A sushi restaurant?"

"People kept mistaking me for someone from the land of sushi, so in the end, I started playing that role myself."

"You could have told them they were wrong."

"I enjoyed being misidentified."

"Why?"

"I got bored talking about being an Eskimo. But it was fun answering questions about a country that wasn't my own. So I decided to act as if I was from that other country, and changed my name to Tenzo."

"But that's no reason to give throw the university over. You wanted to be a doctor, didn't you?"

"Actually, I never really wanted to study medicine. That's just what the people around me thought. For a while it seemed like biology was my field. I was interested in studying about sea otters and whales. But in a big city like Copenhagen, sea creatures weren't really part of my life anymore. So then I started thinking maybe I'd major in environmental biology, or marine science, and study about the fish and seaweed people eat. Studying sea otters and the fish they eat isn't so different from studying people and the sushi they eat. Only with human beings, you can't rely just on what you see. Flavor is important, too, and when I tried to figure out how to bring that into academic research, I started getting interested in studying dashi."

I sensed instinctively that Nanook was lying. Maybe lying isn't the right word, but he was definitely using words as a kind of shovel, to dig himself out of a hole. Sometimes when you do that you find years later that the escape route you dug for yourself that time, in desperation, has become the basis for your research. And when that happens, it's no longer a lie. So right now, while Nanook was talking, it was still too early to tell whether he was in fact lying or not.

"I'd gotten so confused that I didn't know what I wanted to do anymore," he went on, "and all I could think about was getting away somewhere."

"Why didn't you tell me all this? I was all for your plan to go traveling, and if you wanted to study biology instead of medicine, I wouldn't mind. Your major is something you should choose yourself." My mother's voice had lost its accusing tone; she was even starting to sound a little sentimental.

"I wasn't planning to quit the university. But once I started traveling, I crossed the border."

"What border?"

"From Denmark into Germany."

"There's hardly a border there anymore."

"That wasn't true for me, though. Leaving Denmark meant

I cut my ties to Greenland, too, and, like a kite with a broken string, I was free and lonely."

Hiruko giggled again, and my mother glared at her. I couldn't bear to sit there watching her pepper Nanook with questions anymore.

"Don't try to tell me that paying his way gives you the right to force him to follow your plan for him. In Denmark parents aren't allowed to decide their children's future, but you think you can treat someone from a former colony that way?"

My mother suddenly pointed her nose straight up like a fish yanked out of the water on a fishing line. "You're just jealous of your younger brother because I haven't been paying you as much attention as I used to," she said, delivering a punch from an unexpected direction. Smelling blood in back of my nose, I gritted my teeth. Hiruko then quietly stood up and put her hand over my mouth. She probably wanted to keep any words that would cause irreversible damage from getting out. Her hand was delicate, with thin, cold fingers. I gently slid my tongue between the first two. Showing my mother that Hiruko was now the most important woman in my life might be the strongest counterpunch I could deliver. The minute that thought came into my mind, my anger faded away and I started to enjoy myself again.

Just then the door opened, letting light pour in from outside. The huge butterfly wing I thought I saw was the door flapping, dyed white in the sunlight the moment Nora stepped through it, looking like a cutout against the bustling city street behind her. She was wearing a green, sleeveless dress that showed her tanned, muscular arms and legs, completely transforming the image I'd had of her in Trier. Heat and bright light were enough to change her from a museum curator into a nude model stretched out in a spring field.

She looked at each of our faces, not sure who she should

speak to first, but when she saw a stranger—my mother—she stretched out her hand and politely introduced herself in English.

"How do you do. My name is Nora, and I live in Trier."

Looking over at me, my mother said bitterly, "Another member of your international research team, I assume," as if to let me know how much she resented being the only one in the world we'd excluded. She then turned to Nora.

"I am Knut's mother," she said in English. "I am also Nanook's sponsor. I have been worried about him ever since he went missing, and when I came here to meet my son, I was most surprised to find him here as well." She explained this not out of kindness, but to let Nora know that both Nanook and I belonged to her, and to warn her to keep her hands off both of us. Shocked, Nora looked over at Nanook, but as he quickly turned away she trained her eyes on me with a harsh, questioning stare. I shrugged my shoulders. Realizing, perhaps, that she had nothing to accuse me of, she then turned back to Nanook.

"It's not just me—you're running away from lots of people, aren't you?" Nora said. "But why? What is it you want to do? Or to avoid doing?"

Barely stopping to breathe, Nora continued to censure Nanook in German. My mother, who could understand German but didn't speak it well enough to join in, looked disgruntled, her lips opening and closing like a goldfish. As Nanook now seemed more like my alter ego than a younger brother, I wanted to step in and stop Nora's unilateral attack, but if I spoke English I'd be like an American warship intervening in a dispute between two northern European countries. I wished I could speak to Nora in elegant German, but I'd only learned German at school and was afraid I'd sound childish. In English I could get away from childhood, and be cool and collected. But then how to get rid of that "I represent democracy and all that's right" sort of mask that comes with English? I needed to sound clumsier, more desperate, as if this were my last chance—

"Nora," I said, "you and my mother are like a couple of drag-
ons. Attacking Nanook makes no sense. So cut it out, why don't
you. He isn't running away, he's looking for something. We all
are. He's the one who brought us here. Nora, how come you
came all the way to Arles when Hiruko's native language means
nothing to you?"

"I'm not sure myself."

"See—I bet I'm right. You're looking for something. But not
for Nanook, something else."

I was frantic, my spittle flying. I'd just set out on an exciting
journey in search of a lost language and didn't want to get caught
up in a "why did you leave me?" kind of boy-girl spat that might
ruin everything.

"Anyway, why don't you sit down?" I said, dragging another
chair over from the next table for Nora. With six chairs around
the table, my mother didn't look so out of place. But now she and
Nora made up a separate, entirely new category. She didn't seem
to see Nora as an ally, though, the way she was coolly observing
her. She probably suspected Nora of luring Nanook away from
the path of righteousness. That would make Nanook the inno-
.cent lamb, and Nora the one to blame.

"Do you know Nanook well?"

I was a little relieved to hear her ask that out loud, and in English, too.

"I am Nanook's lover."

Nanook shot Nora a surprised look. A sticky sort of smile
on her face, my mother looked around, intently examining our
faces.

"I see, so there are two couples in your group. Nanook and
Nora. Hiruko and that man who I assume comes from her country."

It took me several seconds to understand the chemical chart
my mother had just created, with two pairs of atoms, each fitting
neatly together. When I started to object, she put out a hand

to stop me and pointed her chin toward Hiruko and Susanoo. "Those two go together naturally," she said in Danish. "Unlike Nanook and Nora. He looks like a young boy with a middle-aged woman. As if she'd seduced him and made him her lover."

Unable to understand, Nora looked pleadingly at Nanook. Flustered, Nanook looked to me for help. That's when it dawned on me that my mother's having forced these two couples together left her with me, hanging on the outside.

"Since we're both third wheels," I said, joking to hide my anger, "why don't we just go home together, hand in hand? Traveling together probably isn't such a good idea, though, seeing as you're a much older woman." My mother was unfazed.

"You've been a dimwit ever since you were little. When there were two people in love, it never occurred to you to get up and leave so they could be alone. You always stuck around, making a nuisance of yourself. You never saw yourself as a third wheel."

Hiruko looked at my mother.

"misunderstanding," she said with the directness of Panska. "susanoo and i today first meeting. not lovers."

My mother pretended not to hear her, so I got up, walked around behind Hiruko's chair, put my arms around her neck and kissed her on the ear. Her hair smelled like camellias, though that may have been because *La dame aux camélias* had just popped into my head. Out of a corner of my eye, I saw my mother turning away. When Hiruko tilted her head back to look up at me, my lips pressed against her eyelid.

Just then, the door opened with a burst of color and Akash, dressed in a sari of pomegranate red, burst into the restaurant. I heard trumpets announcing the appearance of a leading actress. Or that's what I thought until I realized it was someone's cell phone ringing outside. Dumbfounded, my mother examined Akash from the top of his head to his feet. The sight of an Indian shouldn't have surprised a cosmopolitan woman living in Copenhagen, and this couldn't have been the first time she'd seen a man dressed in women's clothes.

"I am Akash, delighted to meet you," he said politely, charmingly even, to this strange woman standing in front of him, blocking his way, but my mother, waving her hand as if to wipe his name away, asked, "What are you?" How could she be so rude?

"I am Knut's lover," he answered, not the least bit perturbed. "And you?"

My mother's mouth dropped open. To tell the truth I felt my throat close up and though I normally would have fired back, "What do you mean by that?" I escaped back to my seat to watch him from a distance. He looked just as he always did. With his head tilted to one side, he waited for my mother's response.

Seeing she was so upset she couldn't get even the simplest answer out made me feel much more relaxed.

"This is the person who gave birth to me," I answered in her place, using a verbal phrase in lieu of her title.

"I raised him, too," my mother added, staring menacingly at Hiruko. "You don't understand anything about Knut."

Hiruko laughed like a curtain blowing in the wind. Neither sarcasm nor full-throated attacks upset her. Didn't this strength of hers come from speaking Panska? Though we could understand everything she said in it, Panska always kept its strangeness. Its purpose wasn't to make Hiruko melt into Scandinavian society so that she didn't stand out. And it wasn't directly connected to anyone's native language. As long as she was speaking Panska Hiruko was free to be herself. And since her conversations were like playing catch, she was never lonely.

"So you understand me?" I said to my mother. "I suppose there's a first time for everything."

Because I'd been speaking the same language as my mother since I was a child, I always had the nasty feeling that no matter what I said I'd still be just a part of her. And now she was angry, so I knew she'd say things that would directly attack my nerves. I switched to English before she had the chance.

"Akash, are you my lover? I never noticed till now, but it sounds kind of cool. A little sudden, though, don't you think? I'm only finding out about that now for the very first time, so it'll take some time for me to see if I agree."

I didn't feel like myself somehow, joking this way to the light, airy rhythm of a pop song. His face as slick and smooth as an anime character, Akash replied, "Knut, you don't need a woman. What you've got to have is lots of friends to walk with you. You'll probably never marry. Or have children, either. You are a man of the future, who doesn't need sex."

My mother's face twisted into a nasty frown. "Exactly what kind of group are you?" she asked. "You're not just using linguistic research as a front so you can practice free sex, or some new religion, are you?"

"Akash just said I don't need sex at all, so where do you get the idea we're into free sex?" I shot back. Sex had nothing to do with our group, so how did the conversation end up going in that direction? I blew gusts of irritation out of my nostrils.

Just then, Susanoo floated to his feet like a weightless ghost and started to make a long speech. His mouth opened and closed, his lips pursed and spread, his Adam's apple rose and fell, but I didn't hear his voice. Though she could easily have cut him off, voiceless as he was, even my mother shut her mouth to listen. Nanook looked dazzled, blinking as he watched Susanoo speak. He seemed to be hoping that he, too, would one day be able to talk with such confidence. Hiruko shouldn't have been able to hear him, either, yet she was smiling, and as if she agreed, nodding occasionally. When her eyes met mine, she shrugged her shoulders slightly, as if to say something like, "Isn't it strange how you can understand what he means without hearing his voice?" The thought of taking him to Stockholm to be cured now seemed embarrassing. Susanoo was not sick. He had his own language.

"I see," Akash said suddenly, as if he were reading Susanoo's lips, "you want to go to that place where they're studying loss of speech. If you're going, I'll go with you."

"Akash, can you hear his voice?" I asked. I was jealous, and must have sounded angry.

"You understand, even though you don't hear him," Nora answered in his place, her face shining, and Akash nodded in agreement.

"travel so continues," Hiruko said happily, prompting a deep nod from Nanook. My mother had disappeared from the restaurant.

"Yes let's all go together," I said.